T0209714

AUTOBIOGRAPHY
of a
NEW YORK CITY SALESMAN

My Parallel Life of Transformation
through Conscious Evolution
and Kundalini Energy

RICH MOLLURA

BALBOA.
PRESS
A DIVISION OF HAY HOUSE

Balboa Press books may be ordered through booksellers or by contacting:

Balboa Press
A Division of Hay House
1663 Liberty Drive
Bloomington, IN 47403
www.balboapress.com
1 (877) 407-4847

Because of the dynamic nature of the Internet, any web addresses or links contained in this book may have changed since publication and may no longer be valid. The views expressed in this work are solely those of the author and do not necessarily reflect the views of the publisher, and the publisher hereby disclaims any responsibility for them.

The author of this book does not dispense medical advice or prescribe the use of any technique as a form of treatment for physical, emotional, or medical problems without the advice of a physician, either directly or indirectly. The intent of the author is only to offer information of a general nature to help you in your quest for emotional and spiritual well-being. In the event you use any of the information in this book for yourself, which is your constitutional right, the author and the publisher assume no responsibility for your actions.

Print information available on the last page.

ISBN: 978-1-9822-3174-3 (sc)
ISBN: 978-1-9822-3176-7 (hc)
ISBN: 978-1-9822-3175-0 (e)

Library of Congress Control Number: 2019910114

Balboa Press rev. date: 12/20/2019

To my mother, Gina Mollura, who continues to live in me and my brothers and sister, both in our flesh and blood and in spirit. I also would like to acknowledge my father, Dr. Joseph Mollura, who to this day continues to inspire our family to love life, march forward, and realize our potential in every way possible. Lastly, with every word I have written, I honor my wife, Nancy, and our two children, Jenna and Richard, who have provided me endless joy, happiness, and love through this most extraordinary journey *with* life.

CONTENTS

Kundalini's Sweeping Impact on Emotion
Higher Energies Transform Our Emotional Constitution through
Spirituality, Art, Music, Movies, Theater, Humor, and Relationships

The Intellect's Expansion
Higher Consciousness and Kundalini Energy

ACKNOWLEDGMENTS

It is with the utmost gratitude that I thank the following people for their personal touches that have brought this book to publication. First and foremost, I thank my family for all their love and support. A special note of gratitude to my wife, Nancy, my daughter, Jenna, and son, Richard, for their encouragement and enthusiasm that served as meaningful motivation and added inspiration. Specifically, I would like to thank Rebecca Krauss, our acupuncturist and dear friend, for her deep and profound insight that helped shape the initial vision of the writing to the books completion. I also acknowledge our close friend, Suzan Taylor, for her persistent interest and questions that refined the potential value that the content and ideas could offer others. Very special thanks also to Parthenia Hicks, my editor through KN Literary Arts, for her willingness to delve deep into the ideas of the book so that she was able to help me better communicate and convey the book's ultimate message and purpose. I deeply appreciate the feedback I received in the first version from Christine Valente, Linda Perillo, Sallie Carothers, Derek Hardenson, and Jeff Charno. Their feedback on the first few manuscripts helped form this final and finished work.

A PERSONAL ODE TO LIFE ITSELF WRITTEN MANY YEARS AGO IN MY NOTEBOOKS

Dear Life …

> *I know not what you are …*

> *I know not who you are …*

> *I know, only that …*

> *I love you.*

5 QUOTES FROM ALBERT EINSTEIN THAT HELP GET OUR *CONSCIOUSNESS* GOING IN THE RIGHT DIRECTION . . .

"Ideas and Opinions" by Albert Einstein—c1982, first published in 1954 by Crown Publishers Inc

"What is the meaning of human life, or, for that matter, of the life of any creature? To know an answer to this question means to be religious. You ask: Does it make any sense, then, to pose this question? I answer, the man who regards his own life and that of his fellow-creatures as meaningless is not merely unfortunate but almost disqualified for life" Page 11

*"The most beautiful experience we can have is the mysterious. It is the fundamental emotion which stands at the cradle of true art and true science. Whoever does not know it and can no longer wonder, no longer marvel, is as good as dead, and his eyes are dimmed "*Page 11

His religious feeling takes the form of a rapturous amazement at the harmony of natural law, which reveals an intelligence of such superiority that, compared with it, all the systematic thinking and acting of human beings is an utterly insignificant reflection." Page 40

"How can cosmic and religious feeling be communicated from one person to another, if it can give rise to no definite notion of a God and no theology? In my view, it is the most important function of and science to awaken this feeling and keep it alive in those who are receptive to it" Page 38

"Look into nature, then you will understand it better".

Einstein's words, as recalled by Margot Einstein in a letter to Einstein's biographer, Carl Seelig, dated May 8, 1955. Shortly after Einstein's death. AEA 72-79

INTRODUCTION

How Transformation Came through a Salesman into This Book

Autobiography of a New York City Salesman is about the precious intelligence of life itself and its unstoppable growth through all of creation. It is ultimately about *us*—you, me, and the extraordinary journey that life invites us to explore. The words that follow are for those who hear a mysterious inner voice that speaks of the promise of a higher and more connected existence that we do not yet know or understand. Most people run from this calling and take shelter in what is dependable and familiar; others embrace and welcome the unknown with eagerness, anticipation, and courage. The aim of my book is to excite that living energy in each of us who long for a more interconnected wholeness. The challenge we face is how we pursue such an enticing and potentially fun experience while having to comply with and conform to the responsibility necessary for material survival. Those with such a longing must learn to masterfully weave this deeper calling into everyday life—whether we are home keepers, lawyers, or New York City salesmen. The single most essential element in such a life is not measured by one's external success, but by the evolution of the very consciousness they evolve in this lifetime to experience their existence to its ultimate fullness.

This book isn't about salesmanship, nor is it an autobiography in the traditional sense. While the context of the title will bear itself out, my purpose is to share my experience with those who feel drawn toward this mysterious path, in hopes of opening the unique realm of inner experience that is available to us all. As mentioned above, the steep challenge is learning how to pursue this heartfelt longing in the midst of ordinary life. In my case, I felt a void and emptiness inside that enticed me to seek deeper fulfillment than life offered. I sought an unpredictable way of being that would reverberate *in me* and *with me*. I was lured to the proverbial rabbit hole *in myself* and jumped in. My intention is to communicate this internal journey that has captivated and astonished me over the past forty years. My wish is to help others build an alternative paradigm of inner consciousness that welcomes life experiences as opportunities for internal growth without the conditioned response of labeling them as either good or bad.

My story begins when I was a teenager in Long Island, New York, and traces an inner progression that leads to interconnectivity with the very essence of life that ultimately rewired the very nature that constitutes my being. Throughout these pages, I will explain how this search began, how contact was made with profound eclectic teachers, and, most specifically, how and why I pursued these transcendental aims in a stealth mode while working as a salesman in New York City. I am not writing to convince anyone of any particular perspective, any one particular way of thinking, or certainly any single transformational system, but, as you will see, I have encountered many esoteric traditions and have worked to assimilate multiple teachings and paths along the way. I have since processed these teachings into what I am referring to simply as an *expanded relationship* to life, which I highly recommend for anyone who resonates with any inkling of such a calling. I am hoping that we can take this journey together and invite you to think and add your life experiences and insights as we go, for it is *your* life energy that is most important to the total experience of reading this book.

While I do provide some names of people and places that were part of the search, they serve more to demonstrate how a particular path can unfold and find its way to the great wisdom of life and not to showcase my personal life. In other words, it is the living thread of the consciousness that is important and not the fleeting and inconsequential details. There is profound beauty in following how a searching intelligence navigates its way through life (as yours is doing this very moment reading these words). There is unique music to every journey, and I am hoping my reader turns his or her attention *to their own*, as I did. There is astounding wisdom that awaits those who persist and continue to follow their innermost calling—the potential is a rapturous living relationship with existence that is the ultimate calling for a human being – but each person must open themselves up and take that lonesome journey on. I quoted Albert Einstein five times prior to the introduction because he embodies the adventurous spirit of fascination we need to nourish in order to probe into our life for our higher evolution.

The challenge I face in writing this book is to explain experiences and ideas that may not be familiar to some and a few that have never been heard before. For this reason, I want to start by providing a basis for a shared understanding of what I mean by consciousness, conscious evolution, and Kundalini energy.

Consciousness and Conscious Evolution

From my perspective, consciousness is pure intelligence and is inseparable from our deepest and most intimate sense of who we are. It is the awareness of "I" that we naturally live life from and from which we record and witness existence as we travel through our lives. Consciousness is not limited to mental knowledge or information; it is also not limited to our emotions or even our physical bodies. Consciousness encompasses *all* with an innate and extraordinary awareness that is driven to interconnect everything into one unfathomable higher state. Most astonishingly, it masterfully creates, grows, and expands through the very matter that constitutes all life and, as we shall see, harbors no bounds or limits. It is also important to keep in mind that consciousness extends into matter and matter into consciousness; they are not separate and certainly not at odds. It is one magnificent continuum to awaken to.

The purpose of my book is to explore this great mystery and delve into the ways it can serve as a significant aid to each of us individually. *The core message is that we are all of the same embryonic origin and source of creation and have at our backs this inconceivable force and energy.* It is in the integrity of this masterful genius of creation that I derive my faith, which I find boundless and ultimately unknowable. Of course, this presents a major challenge for all of us because life often appears and feels unfair, harsh, and, difficult—to put it mildly. We are confronted with heartbreaking realities that we often, within our current state of consciousness, can't begin to comprehend. This paradox taunted me for decades as I sought to reconcile these opposites for my own peace of mind. Life, for us, is short, powerful, and perplexing; but then, turn your head—and it is a miraculous wonder! In my book, I refer to a concept I simply call "conscious evolution," which has helped me better grasp this impossible irony of life and evolve toward a higher awareness that has, ultimately, led to the greater personal fulfillment I have sought. By conscious evolution, I mean opening the aperture of our awareness like one does with a camera. This evolution means seeing and perceiving more, *at the same time*. No matter who we are, where we are, or what our personal circumstances appear to be at any given time, our goal is to grow. When growth slows, or evens stops, when we part from that sacred inner space of being alert and attentive in the imminent present, the suffering and trouble begin on all fronts. It is a challenge we face at every stage in life, whether children, adults, or elderly. *Our being needs to be expanding and encompassing more of life together as one total living tapestry.* Our consciousness and our intelligence, in order to not fall prey to suffering, need to use all the circumstances of our personal lives to include and accept existence on a higher plane so as not to fall into the vortex of mental torment. If we can realize the true source of the power that is behind and within us, this potential opens exponentially. Our consciousness needs to be alive, alert, and aware virtually *in real time*—meaning it must be vigilant constantly. My premise is that life needs and wants to evolve, it is its fundamental nature and constitution to do so, and *currently* wants to do this through *us*. But this clearly is not easy and can't be gained solely by reading a book or sitting in meditation. While these practices can certainly help, something much more transformational must occur. A change of consciousness must occur that alters one's state of being and impacts our orientation toward life overall. The one thing that substantiates an increase of consciousness is *connection*. An increase in consciousness means to recognize and make the connection that our experiences are linked and not separate, to remember more of these connections and therefore be able to act from a new and more expanded inner state as a result. An additional dimension to increasing consciousness is not only *to know* things together but *to feel* things together as well. We can learn to feel more things together, which energizes and impassions our understanding. To clarify this point, consider this short and simple hypothetical example I made up:

A person who has a love and kinship for animals might become increasingly conscious of the unnecessary suffering of animals. That coupled with the intellectual awareness of the myriad of negative circumstances that surround animals, both domesticated and in the wild, can generate an action within this person—for example, she may choose to become an animal activist. *Feeling* combined with knowledge can be the catalyst for a new action. This higher level of consciousness connects these two and leads to improved lives for animals (thus evolving the collective consciousness of life itself).

I will be focusing on the potential conscious evolution in us as individuals who are not movie stars or world-renowned contributors to our society (although we are not excluding anyone either) but the everyday people in construction, education, health, and healing or any life vocation we maintain to support ourselves or our family. In other words, "we," the everyday people who may lead silent, though spiritual lives while we get milk and eggs at 7-Eleven before starting our day, often with anxiety and trepidation that accompanies us through this troubling and challenging game of life. Most of us live with a constant neurotic narrative that inflicts our souls; longing to be free from it is, perhaps, the highest aspiration of our inner selves and personal consciousness.

Kundalini Energy

It is important not to be intimidated by the word and concept known as Kundalini energy. Matter of fact, the word and concept was mentioned most popularly in the movie, *Meet the Fockers* by Barbara Streisand who played a Tantric Sex teacher as the mother of Ben Stiller. She implores to her rather aged students: "let's get your Kundalini rising", as she begins her class just before being introduced to Robert De Nero who plays the role of Ben Stiller's potential father-in-law (who is not the most open minded personality archetype). While there are many people who are familiar with this phenomenon, many more are not. Further, it is not well understood even by those who are, and from my point of view, it remains a profound and compelling mystery no matter how we look at it. I also want to be clear from the beginning that I don't claim to understand it either. It is like beholding all of the Seven Wonders of the World at one time because we are touching on the very energy of creation itself. The most pragmatic way to look at Kundalini is as the force of creation and the spirit of creativity *combined*, which is unquestionable and self-evident; no one can say that creation and creativity does not exist. The concept of Kundalini energy dates back to the Upanishads in India in the third century BC. This long lineage entails that it has an enduring history with many levels of understanding and interpretations. While the word may at first sound foreign, it is more immediately relatable as the underlying idea of energy-oriented practices, including the healing arts like acupuncture or physical disciplines like yoga, Tai Chi, or meditation (just to name a few). There is also a far more expansive view of Kundalini, which is what we will explore in the pages to come.

The classic definition of Kundalini is that it is a powerful source of energy that is coiled and dormant at the base of the spine that can awaken and proceed on a course of transformation through energy centers known as chakras. Traditionally, it is taught in yoga and other practices that, in some individuals, this energy can activate and ascend into the brain and cause what many people refer to as enlightenment or a higher level of consciousness. Such a phenomenon would have to impact the individual with inner experiences that challenge what is considered normal. These experiences are rare and therefore would not be readily received by the masses and thus be labeled as either strange or imaginary. While this may be true, it is also true that many human beings experience manifestations of this energy throughout their lives but are not aware that there is a name or a phenomenon behind it. It is so untamed, unruly, and unpredictable that *you* may have experiences of this energy that others have never even heard of before—as I have. We all possess this energy; it is impossible not to. It is also true that extreme Kundalini *activation* is not necessary for one to engage the highest levels of enlightenment, which adds to the mystery. Many great teachers of higher consciousness have no account of Kundalini, and other teachers have had sweeping experiences of Kundalini but chose not to make it the centerpiece of their teaching. Many have felt it impossible to express the nature of Kundalini without creating more confusion or, worse yet, encouraging a delusion of grandeur that distracts the student from true spiritual growth—*the activation of Kundalini does not mean one is enlightened.* What is clear is that logic does not naturally apply to the realms of awakening and enlightenment; it is more like a dream where nothing makes sense, yet it makes sense during the dream itself, and then it does not make sense again when we look with a rational mind. It is vital that we prepare ourselves to be able to leap into possibilities never dreamt of before in order to embrace new orders of reality. A good question for all of us to ask ourselves is whether we are ready to embrace new ideas as drastic as Oz was from Kansas in the *Wizard of Oz.*

I view Kundalini energy as having two dimensions that, while appearing separate, are one. The two dimensions I refer to are my own delineation that I will explain as I recount my personal experience of this overwhelming energy and deliver details that have unfolded over the past four decades. As we shall see, my experience does not follow the traditional model of rising linearly through chakras unless we broaden our definitions and widen our perspective—which we will. Kundalini cannot be limited and can manifest in an endless variety of extraordinary variations unique to every individual.

Thus, the first of the two dimensions I referenced are the unusual *biophysiological experiences.* There are two ways that these extreme experiences can present: they can manifest in sporadic and strange, isolated ways, or it can explode in a full-blown unleashing of this energy over the course of many years. While my experiences can appear extreme (which I will recount in detail), consider your own inner dimensions of higher experience. Specifically, recall the inner extraordinary state of your brain and body when in the throes of an explosive orgasm, or how your whole body feels biochemically when laughing uncontrollably and hysterically, or the extraordinary changes when in an altered state due to a certain type of drug—or better yet, all of them at the same time! Consider that these states are a literal alteration of *your own bio-neurochemistry.* A higher collective energy feels unlocked, even if only temporarily, and you are immersed in rapture. Note that the body harbors these potentials but only need to be catalyzed in a certain way to be experienced. Many people favor the use of drugs because it is the fast and easy route to alter their brain chemistry to a preferred state, as opposed to considering the science of higher consciousness, which seeks to alter brain chemistry intentionally. Ask yourself if you have ever consciously sought to deliberately increase the frequency and intensity of your own higher states of being and consciousness. That is part of Kundalini, but it has correlated experiences in the emotions and the mind as well. In this regard, consider the inner wondrous electrochemical state while communing with nature as in watching a sunset or a beautiful animal; or consider the intense energy in your body and brain while intellectually immersed in exploring something new, learning something new, or realizing a new connection; consider and think about the nature of the inner state of a person while creating art or music or immersed in a favorite hobby. My personal favorite, as we will visit later in the book, is specifically how listening to music alters one's brain and body chemistry and creates a high that few people even notice. All of these physical, emotional, and intellectual experiences have corresponding energy and intelligence at their source. This inner nature is constituted in science and evolution, the potential of which is mind shattering. The key is not to simply hear my words about these experiences *but to stop and observe them in yourself;* we ought to remember that in order to stay warm, we must kindle our own fire and not read about someone else's fire. I also want to add that I fully understand that science explains many of these higher states in terms of bioneurochemistry, endorphins, and so on. They would say that it is not energy; it is physiology. The truth of the matter is that it is both. Take energy out of the body and try to explain hormones. More importantly, it is the intelligence and architecture of the total living design and the extraordinary interconnectivity that accounts for Kundalini the way I understand it.

It follows then that the second dimension of Kundalini is to comprehend this energy as *the underlying force of creation both in nature and in humankind.* From this perspective, Kundalini is the wondrous energy that is transforming everything and everyone around us. It is the energy of evolution and creation, and it is on a relentless journey to grow and expand. This energy is alive and is acting in real time. Just like we do not actually feel blood circulating through our bodies, we don't feel energy moving through our body either, and therefore we question whether it exists and whether it has a nature of its own. The difference is that we can see blood; we can't see energy—yet. But can anyone question whether we are pervaded with living energy? Whether energy fills every cell of our bodies? Just recall an image of a corpse and ask, What is missing? Further, wouldn't this energy *have to* embody a highly ingenious and supreme science in order to animate our bodies with life? And wouldn't this inconceivable science be present in all creation and nature? Thus, Kundalini is the experiences one may have but is simultaneously the same energy of creation that roars through all nature and human creativity from the most expansive of views.

Through the vehicle of my book, I am hoping to appeal to others like me who have also been stirred by an invisible yet compelling inner force that seeks the ever-elusive "something more" that is at the heart of all spirituality. For me, *spirituality is a state of awe that compels action toward a higher aim.* The successful alignment with life can electrify each of us in our own way. My hope is that others will join in this celebration of life and generate a deep sense of gratitude and optimism that can propel us into the next stage of conscious evolution, which promises growth, joy, and a new state of higher being. Please do remember that we all have Kundalini pervading our bodies as living creativity, but it may or may not have a physical activation that throws us against the wall. This is a very important point to consider when reading this book. Your journey may include a profound emotional evolution or enlightenment of consciousness in your brain, without the activation. In life, everything is possible.

My Book's Organization

Autobiography of New York City Salesman is organized into four sections that describe, as mentioned above, my journey while focusing on consciousness, conscious evolution, and Kundalini energy. My personal story is partly interwoven in this book only to exemplify the process and nature of this transformation. Thus, the book is about consciousness and energy, not about me.

In the first section, titled "At Seventeen, the Beginning of a Lifelong Odyssey," I outline my search and the subsequent stages of struggle to fill the inner void and yearning inside me. I detail the teachings that shaped the eventual inner practices I use, address the challenges of applying these ideas to everyday life, and explore the dramatic internal transformation that results: a creative and exciting inner and outer life. To intentionally generate and manifest a higher life takes heart, energy, and action, as is evidenced in this section.

In the second section, called "A Sense of the Miraculous," I highlight the ways my search evolved into a distinct relationship to nature's infinite intelligence as the Kundalini energy ignited my nervous system and inspired a most welcomed comradery with the very extraordinary being of life itself. In this section, I visit nature, wisdom, and technology as the ways in which life incarnates in ever-new manifestations of intelligence. These revelations lead to the way they impacted my understanding of human nature and changed how I met with the most challenging of life's ordeals, from anxiety, to anger, to grief.

In the third section, "Kundalini: Explosive, Intelligent, and Endearing," I flesh out the detail of my full-blown Kundalini experience and activation. My original objective of writing this book was to convey this inner experience of Kundalini; however, as I wrote, I realized that would be impossible without also including the significant highlights of my personal story. Without the experiences of everyday life and how this all interconnected, this book would simply become a list—a description of Kundalini energy experiences (of which there are many books that have already been written). I realized that I could not convey the full truth of the experience without showing my reader how my life was affected by these experiences. I had to be vulnerable and bring out the Kundalini initiate who was hiding behind the salesman. I had to reveal what it was like to live as a son, husband, father and professional who was secretly undergoing sweeping inner change—some of which frightened me to the core—before I began to understand what was happening.

In the final section, called "Wrapping Up Spider Webs, Physiology, and Consciousness," I openly speculate on my experience and this life in its entirety, in hope of offering enjoyable possibilities and visions for a potential future for some or even a small part of humanity. I address specific possible changes and options that may be considered while commuting to and from work, listening to a comedian for simple joy and entertainment, or thinking about the most recent resistance to sudden and uninvited changes that appeared in my life. The book ultimately visits very specific life experiences that include how we addressed our son's Celiac and Crohn's diagnosis and treatments to the most crushing of my life experiences, which was losing my mother to a glioblastoma. It was important to me to bring the core of the book to the day-to-day life hardships in order to highlight the value of the message.

I thank you for joining me on this adventure and hope it inspires growth for you on any level that enriches *your life*. Be prepared to hear about teachers of higher consciousness that you may not have heard of and teachings that at first might sound obscure and unfamiliar. Also, be ready to embrace manifestations of the human body that you may question and doubt but hopefully will allure and intrigue. What I find spectacular is that we cannot help being part of a miracle that we did not create, and the only injustice we do to ourselves is *to not* explore this unlikely mystery of life and Kundalini. The last caveat that needs to be addressed before we begin is to keep in mind that life is over four billion years old, but humankind and recorded history, in particular, is only a fraction of that, which means we need to exercise patience and understanding with one another. Humanity is evolving out of infancy. We shouldn't be surprised when different groups of people have very different interpretations than others and appear very narrow and closed-minded. If we ourselves cannot *listen* carefully to others, then *we* are lost in that same self-ignorance. More importantly, we must see the different fragments in ourselves *first*, since what manifests in others is usually in us as well.

If I were to summarize the ever-changing view I currently hold regarding everything you are about to read and distill it, it would read something like this:

This book suggests that there is an extraordinary and brilliant intelligence in life that is growing, evolving, and exploring existence through all creation. This infinite intelligence is expanding through everything in the universe, through nature overall, and through humanity on earth now. This intelligence operates through our nervous system, muscles, and biochemistry. Our conscious intelligence appears to serve as the mechanism that generates the vision of that neo-evolution but is inseparably connected to the very tissue of our bodies. In essence, the energetic intelligence working through the nervous system is literally the physical manifestation of this evolution. It is cellular and visceral, not theoretical and subjective. The aim for each of us is to embark on our own personal and unique exploration in order to contribute to what one great teacher, Jan Cox, referred to as "the body of Life itself."

SECTION I

At Seventeen, the Beginning
of a Lifelong Odyssey

I was twenty-five years old, driving my car on a road I had driven many times before, when what felt like an electrical shock shot through my body. Though my attention was quickly drawn to this startling event, surprisingly, I immediately assimilated it into my experience and continued on my way, almost as though it had never happened. What I didn't know at the time was that this was the beginning of a fascinating phenomenon that would radically impact the rest of my life. It occurred seven years after I first started on my inner journey at seventeen. At that time, one simple question ignited my search: where does life ultimately lead?

When I try to remember what initially stirred this straightforward question, it's hard to be sure. There were certainly no major tragedies, losses, or unfortunate circumstances in particular. By most measures, I actually had an ideal and secure life. I grew up the middle child of five children; my parents were warm and caring and provided everything we needed, and we never suffered any financial hardships. As a boy, I was typical — carefree and joyful. I played sports, was actually a bit of a clown, and did not do well in school. I found myself mostly in remedial classes (classes for slow learners) and hardly ever read my assignments, did homework, or excelled academically in any way. By the time I was in high school, I had no particular vocation in mind, although I did start playing guitar at fifteen years old. Music would come to play a major role in my life, as I took to the guitar like fire. I became fairly competent quickly because I

1

loved it and practiced often since I didn't spend time on schoolwork. One important note and observation about my guitar playing that would become a harbinger of my future was that I did not learn to read music. I connected to the spontaneity, the creativity, and the experience of improvising. As my interest in music deepened, I became more introspective and withdrawn, but I enjoyed a sense of inner accomplishment and pride from my guitar playing that compensated for the feelings of inferiority I felt at school. Soon after I learned to play the guitar, my brother and I formed a band with a close family friend who played drums and who was quite popular in his high school in the next town over, Manhasset. We added another friend from his high school, who played guitar and sang, and we had our band called The SERJ (*Steve Schiavello, Eric Neher, Rich and Joe Mollura*). For one year, we had a ball; we played at parties, we played at clubs, and our jam sessions and practices were a source of fun and laughter. We were popular and enjoyed ourselves—perhaps a little too much. But this was all very short-lived. The guys in Manhasset graduated, and everyone went their separate ways. I still had two years in high school and was left very much alone because all my social connections had been through the band. This was an emotional transition for me, as I continued to be inept at school, where I had only one friend. I found myself spending an enormous time alone, which ultimately resulted in my forming a firm bond with myself and a deepening appreciation of life and nature, which we will visit later on. A desire to set out on a search for answers in order to alleviate an inner yearning was building in me, but I had no idea what the search was about exactly or where it might lead. I hadn't yet run into the question of where life leads; I was moving to the next stage of my journey.

It was at this juncture in time, when I was seventeen that my one friend at school helped change my life and set me off on a course that would lead ultimately to the writing of this book almost forty years later. His name was Jordan Najjar. He was an avid student of karate and attended a school in our town. I can remember like it was yesterday when we first went to a park near his house and he started demonstrated this art. I remember feeling filled with awe as he practically transformed from the friend I knew to this frightening menace of a fighting machine. He was very advanced and extremely good at it, and, similar to my experience with the guitar, I took to the concept of it with passion and intensity. I wanted to learn this art and asked where his school was. He innocently said that his school was in his temple, and he invited me to a class to observe and inquire about attending, which I did. Later that week, I went to a class not to practice but to simply observe. Again, I was entranced by the level of discipline, the powerful energy, and the entire aura of the atmosphere. There was one little obstacle that my friend and I didn't realize: the school was part of a Jewish temple, and while he was Jewish, I was not. The teacher warmly explained to my friend that while they had nothing against non-Jewish people, the karate school was part of the temple and I wouldn't be able to join their school. While at first disappointed, I went home to the yellow pages and looked up karate schools in my area. This, without knowing it, was perhaps the most pivotal moment in my life, as you will see.

In the yellow pages, I found the Institute for Self-Development, which, coincidently, was in that same next town over, Manhasset. This school taught karate but also taught Tai Chi Chuan and Hatha Yoga. I started taking karate classes about three times a week, but over the next few months, I began realizing that this school was no ordinary school (and that is putting it lightly). In addition to the teaching of physical arts, this school also included a Holistic Health Center where most of these same karate teachers practiced acupuncture and massage therapy, prescribed herbal treatments, and offered a host of other healing treatments for patients. It was state-of-the-art, impeccably managed, and had a distinct sense and feeling of being organized for one unified purpose (which it was)—but more on that later. This all occurred in 1978, and integrative or holistic health was not at all popular or well known.

Around this time, I was about to graduate from high school and had to start finding a direction in life. Not being scholastic, I didn't take SATs or any other standardized test for college. My father suggested that I apply to a local community college that had low standards of acceptance; it might serve to help me find a vocation. It was now 1979, and I had been accepted to Queensborough Community College, which is a two-year college that was only about twenty minutes from my home.

In the year I was enrolled at Queensborough Community College and attending the Institute for Self-Development for karate lessons, a major change began to take place for me intellectually. I was enrolled in very basic (again remedial) courses when suddenly my intellectual disposition began to change entirely. A determination to learn grew inside me. At first, it was all about simply learning to be a good student, improve grades, and establish basic reading and writing skills. As this interest in academics grew, it became extreme. I spent the majority of my time studying and started developing an interest in psychology. I happened to stumble on the book called *Your Erroneous Zones* by Wayne Dyer, which was first published in 1976. This book, which ultimately became one of the best-selling self-help books of all time, struck a major chord in me and introduced me to the work of Abraham Maslow. Maslow was a psychologist who dedicated his research and writings to the study of extremely healthy, internally fulfilled, self-actualizing people, as opposed to the studies of psychological problems, abnormalities, and deviant behavior. I was drawn to these ideas and became engrossed in the concept of human potential—specifically, how one would cultivate higher experiential levels in oneself. My interest in Maslow led to the study of the transcendentalists, namely Ralph Waldo Emerson, Walt Whitman, and Henry David Thoreau. I was filled with an enlivened drive to apply their ideas and teachings into one state of higher understanding in myself. I realized that I did not want to simply enjoy the reading of their words but longed to *experience* the inner states that the words were evoking.

It was then about 1980, and another overwhelming influence appeared for me, this time on TV. I had been particularly interested in the innovative programming on our local educational channel. A new program, *Cosmos* by Dr. Carl Sagan from Cornell University, had been announced. I knew nothing of Carl Sagan until the series started but was engrossed the moment the music started, the images of the cosmos appeared, and his voice broke out in his signature fashion with the words, "The cosmos is all that is, or ever was, or ever will be ..."

In the opening minutes of the first episode, images of the cosmos were presented, which segued into a slow-motion clip of the waves of the ocean as Carl Sagan appeared from a distance, surrounded by land, wind, and sea. He then delivered a perspective that hooked and compelled me like nothing I'd ever experienced before. He was not only the perfect teacher with the rare gift of simplifying the complex, but he exuded wonderment, awe, and adoration for life and the cosmos that I immediately identified with. His respect and love of life resonated with me and helped me connect to my own experience in a deeper and more explorative manner. He articulated profound scientific detail, pondered the extraordinary implications, and then invited the viewer to fully enjoy and participate in what would become for me the ultimate internal experience of connecting information to realization. My search had become irreversible and intensely emotional.

I was now simultaneously working on the body via the physical arts and this newfound intellectual awakening. I was drawn to the ideas of "higher emotions" through the allure of *Cosmos,* and I pursued psychology and Eastern philosophy. In addition, I was becoming more intellectually curious about self-improvement and conscious evolution. About a year into this new life direction, that nagging question made its first appearance in my mind: *where does human life lead?*

This question soon became more refined: *what is the ultimate potential of human experience and how can I make the most of this rather strange yet beautiful thing called life?*

This mental line of questioning would become a significant part of my forthcoming experiences. For me personally, this marked the beginning of a new stage whereby my mind became absorbed in a search for *something more.* In retrospect, when I ask myself why this question arose in me, I can only respond by saying that people are born with an innate gravitas, an inner wiring, that when it meets with life, it unfolds and generates specific karma that drives the person in certain directions. As I mentioned earlier, I hadn't had a difficult life from an external perspective, but something lurked and troubled me deep down. All I can remember is that while I was experiencing an inner flourishing, I was also angered and bothered by the fact that others did not share this experience, and I felt alone with my mind. Many people were quite disillusioned and disgruntled with life. This fact compelled me, even more, to try to understand the nature of higher experience as I questioned how it could be that some people could be so optimistic, filled with joy and excitement, and live such rich and fruitful lives, while others were bitterly angry and depressed. I felt this was unjust and horrifying. Around this time, I came upon what would become a cherished book for me—the classic by William James—*Varieties of Religious Experience.* In this book, I found an extraordinarily wide-ranging description of human experience that lit up my understanding. James wrote with such elite prose, depicting the full range of human experience from what he called "The Sick Soul" to the most astounding mystical and transformative experiences that he found over the course of human history. This brought my question into focus as I came to a more expansive understanding of just how wide the path of human experience can range. His book also alerted me to the perplexing fact that while some people can undergo dramatic change as in a mystical conversion, others remain hopelessly lost to despair and anxiety. For some reason, this reality incensed me, and I couldn't say why. I wanted to defend the good in life and rail against all human experience that caused innocent suffering and what I came to call "existential depression." Another important revelation was that I was uncomfortably aware that these same states were all within me. *This was a critical realization.*

At this juncture in time, while engaged in the Institute of Self-Development and now fully immersed in an inner search for this something more, I eventually transferred to Fordham University in the Bronx. Fordham is a Jesuit school that had course requirements in theology and philosophy, which fed directly into the existential questioning that had already permeated and was now dominating my thought. Exposure to Greek philosophy, Western philosophy, along with a deeper study of the teachings in the Gospels, were juxtaposed in my mind with some of the Eastern teachings I was encountering in the practice and study of Tai Chi Chaun, yoga, and karate. These two very different philosophical traditions were also being assimilated into my growing interest in human potential, making for a very complex mixture of ideas to think about, consider, and ponder.

I was now twenty-one years old, fully immersed in this existential search and quickly vetting through many of the conventional writers, teachers, and thinkers of the past relative to the question of where life ultimate leads and what lies within the potential of human experience. I spent the majority of my time taking long walks, enjoying solitude, and experiencing a very deep revelatory relationship with nature and life. This was extremely enjoyable and engaging, and while I spent a lot of time alone, I was always close to my rather large family and the people at the Institute for Self-Development. Also continuing to grow within me was that unmistakable and restless longing that was not being fulfilled by ordinary information. The so-called answers that were offered by traditional thinking, dogmas, and beliefs were falling desperately short for me. There was inner unrest and feeling that something continued to elude me even while these elaborate ideas were so engaging and inspiring. This probing curiosity was now the heart and spirit of my daily life.

At about this time, a rather surprising and strange thing happened that would shape where my story leads next. As I said, I had been attending karate and yoga classes at the Institute for Self-Development and gradually learning that the school was not an ordinary school. There was something mysterious about the people who ran it, the apparent hierarchy that existed within it, and the fact that there was one teacher, Dr. Robert C. Sohn, who was the founder and originator of the entire organization. Though his name was often referenced as the teacher who taught all the instructors, he was rarely seen by the karate students when I first started to attend classes. I soon learned that he was not only the master of the karate and Tai Chi program but was also an acupuncturist and an herbalist and advanced in many meditative and healing practices. He had written several books and was married to a woman named Tina Sohn, who was an advanced healer from Korea who brought Amma therapy to the United States. Together they had founded and directed the Institute for Self-Development.

My growing interest in existential psychology and philosophy led me naturally to ask more questions about Dr. Sohn and the school (which I had been attending all along). It was explained to me that most of the instructors, therapists, and administrators of the school lived in a house, which I came to understand was an ashram, and Dr. Sohn was actually a teacher of esoteric conscious evolution. For those not familiar with the term *ashram*, it's a communal place of living for people who are working toward a spiritual aim. This is a drastically different way of life in which one doesn't have ownership in the home or pay rent. People live and work for the organization that supports the residence they live in. If you become fully committed, you are not paid a salary and basically surrender your material life to the organization, which pays for everything. The fact that there was an ashram hidden in the North Shore of Long Island couldn't have been more absurd and divergent from what one might expect from this rather affluent and well-to-do area. This served as a slight shock to me, my parents, and the people I knew; it couldn't have been more alien and crazy. The stigma of a cult became pervasive and explaining the ashram to people became exhausting and impossible. But even so, I couldn't defy my own search; that was not an option. However, I, too, sometimes questioned this bizarre concept that was certainly not a part of our culture. While defending it, I simultaneously asked myself and questioned, *Is this a cult? Do I see myself joining such a way of life?* More importantly, I questioned, *what is a teacher of conscious evolution?* This was all quite exciting for me to figure out and was a revelation that catalyzed energy and wonderment in my young self.

This was also the break-off point for me from ordinary, so-called self-help psychology and the beginning of my journey toward an idea of awakening by increasing consciousness. All journeys toward enlightenment are a form of conscious evolution, and conscious evolution is a very different concept from learning how to improve one's self-esteem, live more confidently, or improve one's memory. The answer to the question of what conscious evolution references is one that, although it has a rich history and plays a direct and inseparable role in almost all human life, is the most esoteric of ideas and yet happens to be interwoven deeply into the fabric of everyday life. From this viewpoint, most, if not all, of the teachings of the major religions and some moral and philosophic systems come from a similar source. Consider for a moment that teachers like Jesus, Buddha, Lao Tzu, and many others were among the most highly evolved, conscious beings who taught how to raise one's level of consciousness to a new state of inner liberation and harmonious peace of mind. Envision the possibility that individual human beings all have the potential to grow vertically within their lifetime and evolve toward this same higher level of being. This idea and goal have nothing at all to do with knowledge, reputation, external success, or compliance with external rules and beliefs. Growing vertically means you evolve into a higher level of being in that you become more centered, aware of yourself, and empathetic toward others and life itself. This level of consciousness has all to do with the silent being we each are at the core of our sense of I—that which is aware of a thought while not being the thought. It is that which *feels itself* as being alive and apart from the person we play in life—that which is at the center of all meditation, wisdom, and inner freedom, in the deepest sense of the word. Simply put, if a thought or voice speaks in your head, and *you* hear it, it is that which can hear the thought that can become free of all thought—good or bad. It is this other intelligence that can guide us to a higher and more sound and peaceful existence, *if* we continue to differentiate and become more conscious through self-observation.

The specific book that ignited my mind and was recommended by Dr. Sohn's school was *In Search of the Miraculous*, written by P. D. Ouspensky, which was centered in the teachings of George Gurdjieff (1866–1949). Gurdjieff was a Russian mystic/teacher who not only self-evolved an extraordinary inner life but also communicated teaching that was elaborate and unconventional. One of his core teachings was that humanity exists in a state of sleep relative to other inner states of human consciousness and that his teachings (and other esoteric such teachings) could, with the right efforts, help students raise the level of their own consciousness and awaken. One can spend decades reading and learning about Gurdjieff's teachings and his legacy, but for the purposes of my book, the key contribution was a system he referred to as the Fourth Way. The Fourth Way refers to the practice of evolving higher consciousness while participating in ordinary everyday life. This is vastly different from separating oneself from society and becoming a monk or living as a rebel and separating oneself from society. The end goal is the same but the means very different. One of Gurdjieff's key terms was "remembering oneself," or "self remembering", and that meant actually being conscious of oneself as a living being with a desire to awaken, while in the midst of jobs, relationships, and hardships. Dr. Sohn published a book called *Transcendental Aim* (no longer in print), which was his term for remembering and sustaining a higher aim throughout all life activities. There were other students of Gurdjieff and Ouspensky, namely Robert S. DeRopp and, most notably for me, Dr. Maurice Nicoll, who also studied with Carl Jung, who provided extraordinary insight, relative to Gurdjieff's system, that was practical and impacted me dramatically.

At the crux of my dual life as a salesman and a student of mysticism is this search for a more awake and enlightened state of consciousness while in the midst of everyday life. This is the most ardent challenge for all people who quietly seek spiritual inner lives while living the ordinary, run-of-the-mill life. Many of us have a dual life; actually, we all do. Maintaining a spiritual aim to improve oneself while living among people who purport no interest in such aspirations is not only common but inevitable and inescapable. I have personally made a science of conscientiously pursuing my inner spiritual aim without telling anyone (at all) for years—a very difficult and frustrating effort for many.

At this place in my story, I was twenty-three years old, consumed by the knowledge of these various spiritual paths, comparing them to other psychological and philosophical ideas, and practicing the physical arts seriously. At about this point, I gained a full understanding of the school I was attending and what it actually offered. To the outside world, it was a place to learn karate, Tai Chi, and yoga while simultaneously offering the services of an advanced Holistic Health Center where people came for various integrative treatments that included a Western medical doctor but emphasized acupuncture, Amma therapy (energy massage therapy), as well as chiropractic, nutritional, and psychological services. At the same time, it was an esoteric school that taught conscious evolution to students who were serious about learning these teachings and even committing their lives to the practice and application of these ideas. The inner school was far more intense than I had originally thought and offered a path to becoming a deeper part of its more esoteric teachings, which included an entirely different series of classes that could lead to entering the ashram (a place where you actually live) and participating in its mission, growth, and outreach to society. The classes outlined Gurdjieff's system but were fully eclectic, meaning the ideas were connected to the spiritual depth of yoga, esoteric Christianity, the Kabbalah of Judaism, Sufism from Islam, and many other teachings that reflected the same goal of conscious evolution. The student who attended all the classes had the option of entering what was called the Full Program. The Full Program was a higher level of commitment that provided the option for students to dedicate most of their time and possibly, as mentioned earlier, the entirety of their life to it. Ultimately, one could surrender one's personal possessions and become part of the school by dedicating one's life to the services of the organization, with the aim of using the experiences to evolve one's own consciousness. That is how it all fits together.

I'm sure it is clear by now that, at that time, this was a most unusual school and that I was finding myself on a quite unanticipated and spontaneous journey. There was still the question of whether it was a cult, whether the intentions of the school were legitimate, and whether I personally would commit myself to lifelong service to the school. I was fascinated by the ideas of esotericism but was also constantly questioning the whole system of ideas that enveloped me. The teachings of Gurdjieff, Ouspensky, and Nicoll were utterly engrossing to me during this time and propelled my inner life. The school was now a vehicle for me, but I wasn't fully sure of what to make or do with it. I also did not yet have a career direction in life. I was graduating from Fordham University and positioned to go into psychology, but the Institute for Self-Development (the school I am speaking of) was offering a much different direction. What was clear to me was that the knowledge coming from the inner circle of esotericism, with its extreme emphasis on higher experience, was what I would be dedicating myself to and was all I could think about. It was anything but a fleeting interest. The deeper question that plagued me through all these decisions was: *What exactly am I looking for?*

The idea of the Fourth Way began to dictate my direction. To be clear and repeat the most important message I hope to impart, the Fourth Way is a path of conscious work on oneself that is applied to oneself while living an ordinary, secular life. The objective is exactly what is taught by some of the most influential teachers today, including Eckhart Tolle, whom I will discuss later and who exemplifies an extraordinary level of this very same awakening taught in this school. Higher consciousness is almost always about living with a very different relationship to the thoughts in our head. This newly evolving level of consciousness has an intelligence that can *encompass* thought and offer an alternative to its hypnotic power over us. While a large part of me was interested in psychology and I considered going into clinical psychology, the alternative direction offered by the Institute of Self-Development was more immediate. At this point, I was drawn to the potential of transformative experience and felt that heavy intellectual engagement in graduate work was not what appealed to me. I wanted to work on my own consciousness because I had a deep-seated desire to explore where it could go. I felt that traditional psychology, although interesting, would lead me further away *from the actual experience* I longed to explore. I wanted to *feel* a difference as opposed to *talking* about a difference. I wanted to *live* from understanding and not remember after the fact how I should have or could have experienced life on a higher level. These teachings of working on oneself were about observing oneself, putting oneself in uncomfortable situations, confronting weakness and limitations, and moving consciously into a new inner frontier that our mechanical existence could not have offered. There was a distinct inner taunting in me that was urging me to watch out; it could be very easy to get lost in life's promises and dreams. I preferred the immediate path, and although I felt I could excel as a psychologist, I was clearly leaning toward this alternative direction. I, however, had no idea how I would make my living, and I did not have the innate desire to move into the health profession that many of the other students of the school were pursuing.

Under the suggestion of the school, I considered getting a job out in the world, moving out of my house with my parents and family, and putting this so-called spiritual aim to work. The traditional Gurdjieff System was very strict about weeding out dreamers and people who fancy themselves as spiritual seekers with no real understanding of what it means. Such people tend to be seeking shelter from life or want to bask in the image of being spiritual. Though it may all sound innocent and harmless, such people do not belong in a school of this kind and ultimately would not be happy. A teacher like Gurdjieff would rather drive such dreamers away than have them suffer in something they didn't bargain for. His system actually used a specific term he called the "good householder" that refers to the fact that students of conscious work must be capable of operating at a functional and successful level in the world before they can realistically profit from inner psychological work. Gurdjieff himself was a master at this, and his life reflected these ideas. He contended that a person would need to be able to handle ordinary life with *their left foot* in order to properly pursue higher consciousness. The core message was that spiritual work and conscious evolution is serious and not to be taken lightly or leisurely. I want to emphasize this point because it is crucial: the idea of a good householder means that a person can hold a job, pay their bills, behave respectfully and responsibly, take care of all basic needs, and be able to manage in life without a lot of drama, complaints, and unnecessary suffering—in other words, one cannot be an immature child that outwardly begrudges life and pursue the aim of higher conscious evolution. Higher aspirations of inner growth demands maturity and discipline not self-hate, self-pity, and escapism. Although one cannot be perfect by any means, the student of transformative psychology needs to have a desire to do things well and have a working strategy to deal with the challenges of life. Life is difficult, challenging, and sometimes downright cold and indifferent. We cannot be babies in grown-up bodies, or life will chew us up and spit us out (to be blunt). I, at this stage, certainly wasn't there yet but had a burning desire to get there. I didn't like the feeling of being an overly dependent, emotionally reactive, mental sourpuss or sorehead, as some like to call such people. I want to emphasize that none of this is easy because it is natural, mechanical, and predictable to whine, be lazy, and therefore become negative and pessimistic. It takes work—*hard work.*

At this juncture in my life, I was unsure if I was a dreamer seeking lofty ideals about becoming more conscious and if I was deluding myself in some psychologically bizarre way. This was an ongoing mental struggle. I felt I was pursuing something quite palpable, but I couldn't be sure what it was. I knew that I felt a distinct emptiness, on the one hand, but was skeptical about where I was going, on the other. The system and teachings of the school compelled me and were driving all my actions. It was at this time that I came to understand that the role I would play in the outside world would become a means to an end and not the end itself; in other words, while I wanted to do something in the outside world that I enjoyed, the more important issue was working on my inner states of consciousness while I performed my job and lived my life. The question was an existential one: *what do I want from existence and how does that differ from what an ordinary life would offer and deliver without this unusual desire?* Another important point is that I did not find all of life lacking in some way. I actually loved life so much that I didn't want it to feel empty in *any* way. I enjoyed people, nature, music, and just about everything that was good in life. I was quite happy and wanted a dimension of life that included, encompassed, and even enhanced what was good in life—not to shun it or deprive myself of it. This is a vital part of the story in regard to living two lives (my dual life): I actually loved both of them—the spiritual journey and my secular everyday life and the ways that the two formed one ultimate personal fulfillment.

I arranged a meeting with the director of the institute to discuss my possible future within the organization. I knew that whatever direction my life would take, it would be driven by this internal goal of conscious evolution. It was clear to me that I could not simply pursue a conventional life and that my inner search was the driving force within me. In retrospect, this was a critical moment, as I opted to suspend all ideas of graduate school and go out and find a job. The question was, a job doing what? The director of the school clearly stated that from the perspective of serious spiritual work, it was not so much the job one performed as much as it was one's internal aim while performing that task or job. The inner work was all about work on oneself in order to see the true nature of one's personality so that one could understand its essence, encompass it, and ultimately transcend it. The student needed to be vigilant while out in the world being a responsible adult and tending to responsibilities of society. The key was to not identify with the role or job—not to get buried in the part or in the thoughts that were so convincing and certain. The idea is to use life experience to catalyze different reactions from the ego, mind, emotions, and body so we can observe them directly and act against them in order to earn freedom from them. To me, this opened the possibility of securing any job that generated an income and allowed me to move from home, take on responsibility, and apply these ideas to my goal.

Not long after the meeting with the director, I had a conversation with another student of the school who was also interested in the internal work and made his living as a salesman. He educated me to the fact that, in sales, one could make more money than most salaried jobs if one could get hired into a good company. Sales also offered a solid opportunity to work on oneself psychologically because the job called for self-discipline and demanded that one constantly be alert and willing to work in continually changing circumstances. I saw this as the perfect challenge since my personality was quite the opposite of a typical salesman and so decided to try it. After several trials and errors from my first interviews and firings, in 1984, at the age of twenty-three, I secured a job at Pitney Bowes in Woodside, Queens, covering parts of Brooklyn, Queens, and Harlem. Pitney Bowes is a Fortune 500 company that is ranked number one in the industry of mailing machines that print postage on envelopes. I found myself in some questionable areas and dangerous neighborhoods, selling postage machines while keeping the intentional aim of working on this idea of conscious evolution. At the same time, I was making deeper commitments to the inner school at the Institute for Self-Development, taking classes, and following their entire course offerings.

The Work

It is important that I review quickly what exactly The Work refers to. One definition might be that it is *the conscious effort to alter one's own consciousness in a way that results in one being less mechanical, automatic, and pre-scripted.* The aim of The Work is to liberate one's consciousness from the conditional fetters of physical, emotional, and intellectual habit that feed the ordinary pattern of suffering in an individual. Our incumbent and birth-given consciousness operates more along the lines of trying to manage external results, events, people, and circumstances to bring about a change in one's life. Simply put, we all try to better ourselves by losing weight, getting a better job, or finding a good partner. It is the if/then logic: if I lose ten pounds, then I will be happier; if I get a better job, then I will be more content; if I find the right partner, then I will be a happier person.

For the most part, we spend our lives chasing many of these ideals with varying levels of success and almost always with a sense of doubt and uncertainty. And even if we do partially succeed, life has a way of changing things, so we always need to be in ready mode toward life, no matter how comfortable things may feel at any given moment. Again, there is absolutely nothing wrong with this disposition, and it is absolutely essential to everyday life, but for a student of The Work, there is a second aim that is fully and completely internal. It runs parallel or simultaneous to ordinary life and is ultimately the search for enlightenment. This is the inner pursuit of all spiritual quests and the many teachers, systems, and schools that exist. It is also the promise of all aspirations to be a better person and human being in general. In a sense, everyone is on a journey to improve their life and reduce suffering, but in most cases, that goal is not distilled into a consciously pursued objective that uses highly specific strategies, practices, and techniques. Most of us are too overwhelmed with life to ever get on firm footing and become grounded and centered enough to make it a permanent presence in our everyday life. The Work is about intentionally living toward that end. The hard part is first finding a teaching to pursue, but the even harder part, and why it is called The Work, is that we must alter, expand, and elevate our consciousness so *we can remember* the aim. The deeper reality that I have learned over a long period is that one needs an enormous amount of energy in one's brain to even remember that we have an inner aim at all.

Back to My Story

Now in the first full year working at Pitney Bowes, I moved into a basement apartment in Bayside Queens and was fully committed to the esoteric school. At this point, I had officially joined what I earlier referred to as the Full Program and was focused on applying the esoteric ideas in my life while developing skills as a salesman, working on both fronts simultaneously. These days started by waking up early in the mornings and practicing Tai Chi, studying esoteric writings, and practicing different methods of meditation before going to work. The goal of my discipline of meditation was to set a distinction between my deeper sense of consciousness and the narrative of mechanical attention. During the day, when I first got my job, and before I transferred to New York City, I was in a driving territory, so I spent a good amount of time in the car. I listened to cassette tapes of talks from the school as well as talks from other teachers from different traditions and perspectives. I would go on a sales call and try to "remember myself" and observe how my personality reacted to rejection, success, and my own incompetence. Self-remembering, as mentioned earlier, is a term derived from the Gurdjieff work, which references the practice of remembering to be aware of yourself in the moment and take note of an observation of your body, emotions, and (or) mind that is used for your self-evolution. The challenge was to apply the self-transformative ideas while in the moment of interactions with customers. The effort was to have my consciousness be aware of my body, emotions, and mind while interacting with people and performing my job. I had developed a habit (which continues to this day) of having a notebook with me at all times so I could write what I observed and develop perspective and insights around those observations. Examples of these observations were largely about observing self-righteousness, indignation, entitlement, and just about every psychological dynamic I could find. I was also surrounded by fellow salespeople in the office who couldn't be more opposite than me. They were not practicing self-observation and pondering the nature of the ego and existence while selling mailing machines. This reality, in a sense, kept me very aware. It served as what is referred to in Gurdjieff's teaching as a *shock*, which generates conscious energy. Again, this idea of a shock is vital; a shock in this context is when your ordinary state of consciousness is suddenly catapulted into highly alert state, as if nothing exists but your awakened consciousness. You may notice that many of us live in a somnific if not comatose state; we drift from one experience to another, not noticing that we ourselves are actually alive. I felt so completely out of place as a salesman that it kept me awake and vigilant to my internal aim. I often felt like I was going in and out of the twilight zone but was fortunate to have a warm noetic awareness that it would all come to fit together—*somehow*. I had a sense that a masterful intelligence was engaging in a strange game of hide-and-seek with me and that it had a playful nature, which we will visit later. The critical takeaway is that I was learning how to use my everyday life, no matter what I was doing, to observe myself and grow in self-awareness. The journey I was on was to live in a higher state of being without being a puppet to external circumstances, so I could experience higher energies of the body, emotions, and mind.

Pondering

Of all the experiences that The Work inspired in me, the practice of pondering was one of the most important in addition to self-observation and Kundalini activation. Pondering was the word that Dr. Sohn used to refer to the practice and effort to think openly, creatively, and productively about oneself in the context of life. Gurdjieff taught that in order to manifest change from psychological work on oneself, the student needed to think about what they were doing and why. The entire work was targeted at not doing things blindly, mechanically, and repetitively without having awareness of it. Pondering and thinking become a central practice because the student is striving to displace the mechanical feed of mental repetition, ongoing complaining, and incessant judgment of others with more productive and valuable content that is driven by the goal to transcend it. Thinking and pondering fed the energy of the aim itself, or else the entire work effort would be forgotten. It became clear to me how easily the entire effort of self-evolution would virtually vanish in a flash of a moment. I was astounded at how I could spend hours engaged in so-called spiritual practices yet be completely oblivious to it a moment later. It was an everyday event to psychologically wake up two to three hours after having a spiritual insight, only to find that I had gone completely on automatic without even a trace of this so-called spiritual practice for that time. My only choice was to press on and definitely not engage in self-hate and self-criticism for more than ten to twenty seconds or the amount of time it took for me to become aware that I was engaging in such counterproductive and useless mental circularity. The goal was to build a conscious awareness so I could be more alert internally while amid external events. As mentioned above, the inner practice could be summarized as having an intention toward inner liberation while simultaneously working toward that objective by observing myself and thinking about those observations in light of that intent. It was now absolutely clear to me that this search was all about one thing, and that was to alter my own consciousness to a more preferred or more favorable state than I was born with (which we all have to define for ourselves). What I was about to find out, though, was that my entire body was about to engage in this effort in a way I could have never expected, which I will explore in detail later. Another quick point relative to the idea of pondering and important to the growth of consciousness was the astonishing and uncanny attribute of many spiritual teachers to speak extemporaneously and spontaneously without notes or reading from teleprompters. This was the case with Gurdjieff and Dr. Sohn from my school, and Jan Cox whom I will speak about later, as well as more well-known teachers like Krishnamurti and Eckhart Tolle (among many others). They all have this in common as the finest example of very advanced pondering that is a bit spooky on a certain level, if you think about it. I marveled at how these teachers could deliver such rich and complex narratives without a planned lecture. Eckhart has made it clear, and has joked about the fact, that he has no idea what he is going to say when he begins to talk at a retreat or speaking engagement. It all simply flows. The enticing question is: How do such wonderfully intelligent musings and insights generate out of the brain without diligent attention prior to the event? And in front of hundreds if not thousands of people, no less! We will explore this intriguing mystery further in the second section of this book. Most importantly, it is whether we openly *think* about our psychological world in a consistent and productive manner throughout our lives relative to a specific purpose. Do we take notice of how selfish we are or how judgmental we are and actually *think* about it and ask, *How am I being selfish? In what other ways am I selfish? Have I observed myself being selfish before? Do I like people who are selfish?* This is an example of pondering things you observe that build this profitable dual life I refer to. It is very important to note though that this is not done with angry self-hate and self-criticism. If the person is whining, complaining, and becoming miserable about what they are observing, then they are clueless to this inner work. It is difficult, and we all fall prey to it often, but all the nonsense in our ordinary mind must be under scrutiny and become drastically reduced or there is no supplemental energy to apply to a higher mind. In a very real sense, we are waging war against self-destruction, which unfortunately comes very natural to humanity. It is our nature to fail in this effort so come to expect it but relentlessly press forward without becoming critical. One must learn to simply observe in silence, add to one's understanding, and have compassion to oneself. Be playful with this effort and don't give in to self-hate and discust (althought you will, repeatedly). Laugh about it, don't whine and cry.

As Life Transitions, Kundalini Fires Her First Shot

I was twenty-one and immersed in The Work and my job. The synergy and activity at the school were teeming, as it was on the cusp of an incredible growth surge. I was one of about ten newer students who were seriously engaged and committed to the Full Program and were part of the school's extraordinary expansion. Around this time, the school started a licensed program that would teach massage therapy and later acupuncture to the public. This was the beginning of what would ultimately become a prominent school in New York known today as the New College of Health Professionals. It was also during this time that I met my future wife, Nancy, who was an assistant manager at the Holistic Health Center I was attending.

It was during this time that the electrical shock I mentioned earlier shot through my body while I was driving. This shock was not my imagination;

it felt as if actual electricity spontaneously fired from my torso and chest through and down my arm. This paranormal experience took me by surprise, of course. What would follow over the long term would be an inner condition that has been morphing and evolving ever since—and becomes *quite* extreme. At that time, I had not heard of Kundalini activation, even though I had been studying and practicing energy-oriented physical practices for more than five years. The idea that an inner energy system underlies the body and is directly correlated to one's health and life was a central tenet of the Holistic Health Center and Institute for Self-Development, but there was no mention of uncanny and unusual manifestations in the body of this kind. In other words, my energy experience was certainly not something that was taught or anticipated. In addition, since my father was a doctor with a Western mind-set, I secretly really didn't believe that energy existed as a palpable, separate dimension of the body. I was biased deep down and skeptical about such an energy field. Yet, as life would have it, there I was engaged in the Holistic Health Center amid healing energy concepts, physical practices based on energy, and spiritual ideas reflective of energy, while deep down, in the most remote parts of my being, I didn't see it and therefore didn't believe it could be so. Yet the unusual experiences that would ultimately electrify my inner body were just beginning.

Before I delve further into the energy experience, a few other major transitional developments took place around that time regarding the direction of the school and my personal experience. First, regarding the school, I, along with the other ten newer students, had taken the next major step of committing ourselves to the organization by moving into the ashram. This was not your traditional ashram. It was a large mansion in a very expensive area of Nassau County Long Island called Muttontown. For just under one year, I lived in this ashram where there were Satsangs (a gathering of students and teacher in a group for meditation or lecture) on Friday nights, Tai Chi every morning, and activities around the house and school that were assigned to each one of us individually. We all wrote personal logs that were meant to keep us alert to what was going on inside ourselves and vigilant to remembering our conscious aspirations. These logs had to be written and handed in daily because they were read by one of the senior instructors and handed back with comments. The instructor would point out how the student was being defensive or delusionary in their perception, or how a pattern was emerging that showed how angry the person was, or how we kept pointing out how life was so unfair. Again, the goal was to become more conscious and to elevate one's level of being by becoming more aware of oneself on a moment-to-moment basis. There was also a collective effort to keep one another awake by reminding each another to self-observe and not get caught up in emotional states or become hopelessly identified with thoughts. There were meetings, confrontations, and constant activities that were assigned to help go against the grain of our personalities and egos, thereby exposing the deeper nature to our evolving consciousness. If it isn't clear by now, the chief and central idea is that our automatic selves tend to be miserable, anxious, selfish, and childish and this inner higher psychology is for people who see and accept that fact but choose to work on transcending it. If a person *prefers* to take refuge in being disgusted, pessimistic, and cynical, then they will attract that karma and stay there for the duration of their lives. Life tends not to rescue people who don't put their shoulder to the wheel.

The so-called confrontations were an interesting phenomenon that merits explanation. A confrontation was actually an act of compassion by an instructor to wake the student out of a mentally asleep state. They were designed to make the student alert to what they were doing but rile their defensive nature at the same time. Being defensive was a form a deep sleep from the perspective of The Work, and I found my personality intensely resistant to such treatment, which meant it was effective for me. It was during this period that I realized just how hostile, lazy, incompetent, and immature I was at the core (all personalities and egos are). It was all quite intense, but the residence at the ashram did not last long. Within one year, significant things started to happen in the hierarchy of the inner school that would negatively impact those of us who had recently made this commitment. While the external school and Holistic Health Center continued to grow, we were unexpectedly thrown into turmoil as the associate director and his wife suddenly broke off from the organization. This associate director was our main teacher because Dr. Sohn had become more removed, leaving this phase of teaching to his students. I found their departure disturbing and realized that after this uncomfortable and mostly unexplained event, I could not devote my life to the school. It is important to understand that a school of this nature is built on the trust and credibility of the hierarchy.

Deep down, I was depending on their integrity to help support my decision by demonstrating a sense of hope and reassurance. I no longer felt the commitment because I was now questioning whether there was something I was missing. That element of doubt convinced me that until I was clear on my resolution, I could not commit my life. I moved out of the ashram, as did most of the other new students, although my passion for spiritual work itself remained unshaken and locked in.

Once out of the ashram, I was still fully committed to inner growth and development and continued to go to classes at the Holistic Health Center. While my relationship with Nancy deepened, I continued to work at Pitney Bowes. After about a year, I felt uncomfortable at the school and decided not to attend any more classes. In retrospect, there was a lot of tension in the air for those of us who moved out of the ashram but still attended classes. The instructors and fully committed members of the ashram were always there, which made me feel a sense of guilt or that I no longer belonged. There were also feelings of personal failure since I couldn't be sure if I had made the right decision. For me, these were very emotional and difficult times because my inner longing and search did not waver at all throughout the turmoil. As a result, my internal efforts became more intense and increasingly private.

The Holistic Health Center continued to grow, with many significant changes taking place. It appeared that the external school was reaching greater numbers of people and teaching hundreds and then thousands of students to become massage therapists and acupuncturists. Eventually, Dr. Sohn and Mrs. Sohn were no longer running the school. As far as I understand, a few of his most devoted students remained involved for many years, but over the long term, new leadership took over, and the entire inner esoteric school was eventually gone without a trace. The organization, as I mentioned earlier, currently known as the New College of Health Professionals, offers accredited degrees in massage therapy, acupuncture, and Oriental medicine, yet makes no mention of the history or its extraordinary origination. To me, it was invaluable and ignited the very experience I'm writing about today. I also need to add that all these sudden and swift changes never shook my inner direction. I never lost focus of my personal aspiration, and it did not weaken the credibility of the teachings I loved. These external dramatics are often a strange part of such teachings and quite common. It is almost an expected reality that people will splinter off due to different levels of being and understanding. It is up to each individual student to weave his or her own web of consciousness despite what happens in the external world. This goes for everyone, whether we become part of such a school or do it alone. The harsher reality is that we are all ultimately alone in this, no matter our story and involvement in an inner spiritual quest. Many people who are drawn to ideas of a spiritual awakening do not have the privilege of finding a school like I had and do what they can to read, meditate, apply the wisdom, and deal with the difficulties on their own. Such people often have to cope with a similar issue in that the people who surround such seekers don't share in their budding interest. This creates another challenge that I will discuss in a future chapter, but notice how this issue is interlaced with my story as it unfolds. In my case, although I was clearly and staunchly pursuing this sublime inner directive, I was surrounded by people who had no such interest whatsoever, including my wife, family, and friends. Many of the people I was close to at the time, to whom I did try to explain the nature of the school and the ashram, thought I was a lunatic (but were nice enough not to say it). My interest in saying a word about it disappeared completely, while the internal richness was unquestionable. I had come to understand the esoteric meaning in the Gospels where it was taught that the kingdom of heaven is within and how a seeker does not need to be *seen of other men*. In other words, if a seeker deeply values inner work, they lose the need to have other people approve or applaud their efforts. I didn't speak of this activity with anyone whatsoever until the writing of this book.

The Parallel Life Begins to Form

As these changes occurred and I adjusted to what looked like a quite different future than I was so conscientiously working toward, a few other developments arose that would dramatically impact me. First, I suddenly went from being a student in an esoteric school, fully engaged in ashrams, yoga, and Satsangs, to a salesman in Queens, soon to be engaged to be married, with no connection to any external manifestations of the teachings that drove me to all this to begin with. Although I kept some contact with some of the other students, we mostly dispersed and went our separate ways. Yet, while we were moving out of the ashram, my closest friend in the school, Jeff Charno, asked if I wanted a box of cassette tapes of talks given by another esoteric teacher who taught a group of people in Atlanta. His brother had been involved in these rather unusual teachings for many years, and the teacher and the teachings were quite astounding. I immediately accepted the rather large box of tapes and some written material he had given me. Little did I know, this teacher would become an extraordinary source of conscious intelligence that would inspire, engage, and provide me with a highly unique inner adventure of conscious revelations that would fuel my interest for decades and up to this very moment. His name was Jan Cox.

This was the period of time during which I established a distinct internal life dedicated to learning more about the system of ideas taught by Jan, while the specific energy experiences (that I discuss in detail in section III) began to unleash in my body. This was also when I moved into an apartment with Nancy and was intent on pursuing an inner life while enjoying my external life to the maximum. As I said earlier, the inner drive to understand what I was searching for not only intensified but transitioned into what I would call an entirely stealth stage. In other words, I pursued this objective on my own with zero external involvement with people, classes, or organizations of any kind relative to esoteric conscious evolution. By this time, my friends, family, and Nancy were all glad I had moved out of the clutches of what appeared to them a cult and were relieved that I had become a "regular" person. I, however, was not very regular internally. An early riser, I started to get up earlier and earlier until it became a habit to wake up at three in the morning, study esoteric texts and transcripts, write in my personal journals, practice Tai Chi and Chi Kung, and take long walks, during which my mind would interconnect ideas, experiences, and observations of myself and life itself (pondering). I became the object of many jokes as Nancy and others thought I was quite weird—which I kind of was (and am). The jokes never bothered me. Honestly, I kind of enjoyed them because it was the only time the secret part of my life got any attention whatsoever, and I loved the growing inner experience so much that it helped fuel the energy inside me.

Eventually, I transferred within Pitney Bowes, from Queens to New York City, benefited from consistent success in sales, got married when I was twenty-eight, had our daughter, Jenna, in 1992 and our son, Richard, in 1998, and embarked on what would become this ever-unfolding, progressive, and quite astonishing integration of consciousness and energy. The transfer to New York City occurred in 1995, the same year we moved into East Meadow Long Island, where we found a house that had an entire upper floor that I made into my office and sacred space. This is where I would spend three hours every morning, prior to getting on a train, delving ever deeper into esoteric content, organizing music and lectures, writing, and practicing yoga and Chi Kung to help balance the energy that I will be discussing later in the book.

The transfer into New York City represented a major challenge to the inner work because I no longer had my car as my place of refuge. My car had been equipped with books, notebooks, and cassette tapes that I would no longer have access to once working in New York City. The city was loud and distracting, making it hard to remember my inner aim. I began carrying a large and heavy briefcase filled with books, a cassette player, and my notebook. My commute to Penn Station was just under fifty minutes, so for at least two hours a day, I was wrapped in what I loved. Once in the city, I had to shift to a second briefcase that I kept under my desk to take out on appointments. In that briefcase, I had a separate personal journal that was lighter in weight, since I needed room for customer files, brochures, and paperwork. I would often write in Central Park, hotel lobbies, libraries, and eventually, largely in Starbucks, which quickly became my favorite refuge and a second home that I would seek everywhere I traveled. My love of Starbucks and how I sought one out every trip also became a source of jokes with family and friends.

Later, as technology evolved, I transferred all my music and extensive files of Jan Cox talks (hundreds of them) into an iPod Classic. I had more than ten thousand songs and lectures and divided them into highly specific playlists that helped me manage my moods and keep my brain filled with esoteric content. Later on, I added talks by Eckhart Tolle and a few other teachers and listened to them while walking through the streets of the city. Walking was my escape from the mundane because I was able to think. I walked practically everywhere unless I was pressed for time. I spaced my calls so I could have time to walk, think, and listen. For me, it was second nature to walk from our office, which was near Penn Station, to Wall Street or Central Park and back daily. That walk was almost ninety minutes and sometimes I made sure I had sales calls along the way that were spaced and scheduled to meet the need of the walk. I also came to have favorite spots in the city to write, eat, and center myself. The years went by as I continued to record experiences, write about them daily, and enjoy a very active life with my kids, wife, family, and friends. From the outside, we couldn't be more ordinary, and as mentioned earlier, I absolutely cherished this life. I enjoyed parenting more than anything, and we enjoyed a very close family connection with both sides of our families. My wife and I both came from two rather large Italian families, so the years were filled with big holiday celebrations and family vacations, and our social life was quite active as well, since my wife loved to socialize, give parties, dance, and have fun—much like my mother. One important note regarding marriage, since it is one of the most complicated challenges to one's ego and personality, is that while studying many deep esoteric and philosophical teachings, I also continued to read books on optimizing everyday life. The series of books by John Gray, which for me started with *Men Are from Mars, Women Are from Venus,* had extraordinary impact. I spent an enormous amount of time integrating his ideas into esoteric self-development. The idea of becoming conscious of how two people can have entirely different *experiences* of the same interaction was ingenious, and the way John articulated it was entertaining and precise. It became customary for me to uncover books and teachers like these to help reduce conflict and enforce optimism and growth in my marriage and with friends. All these efforts helped create a surplus of energy to direct toward higher consciousness. The profit I gained from those self-help books, in addition to the insightful information, was the accumulation of consciousness required to remember the information in the moment. Having a remembrance of one's aim takes positive mental energy, and if the seeker is immersed in conflict, anger, hostility, worry, and fear, there will be no residual energy to work on a higher aim. I think it is a healthy approach in life to take every facet of it, whether it is a relationship, parenting, financial planning, or any part of it and have a progressive approach. Whether through books, lectures, video, and internet; it doesn't matter—we should always be on the alert to see what is wrong and change it for the better. If we wait for life to come to us—*we lose.*

In the second and third sections of the book, I will go a step deeper into the inner world that I explored and traversed as a result of the work

I was doing and the details of the Kundalini energy experience that distinctly unfolded in my body. I will also visit some of the more difficult and challenging times we faced as a family, relative to the inevitable harsh realities of health, aging, and the eventual passing of Nancy's father and my mother. This all comes together to form a perspective and view of life that I hope is helpful to my readers. As will become apparent, life opens up to new revelatory dimensions of itself when we welcome its deepest mysteries.

SECTION II

A Sense of the Miraculous

The Ultimate Teacher Arrives from Virtually Everywhere

Throughout the years that followed, the inner journey never ceased as I continued all the practices mentioned. The electrical shocks became more frequent and more powerful, along with other manifestations that included spontaneous contortions of my body, sudden openings of blissful energy fields from deep within, odd crackling and crunching of nerves (which horrified my wife), changes in breathing, and many other manifestations that I will detail in the next section. All of these experiences were under my conscious control in that I would *almost* never manifest them in public, and if I did, they were intentional. The energy vacillated and oscillated between cycles ranging from low activity to hyperactivity, and at times the energy was so active that I had to find solitude so I could accommodate them by using Chi Kung methods, yoga practices, or a combination of the two, along with my own instinctively improvised techniques that I learned over the years. When I say these Kundalini experiences were erupting, it was like multiple mini volcanoes were firing from different fronts, which I desperately worked to encompass, welcome, and route intuitively. They were stark, authoritative, and unmistakable, and they altered my emotions and mind simultaneously with the body. This was a dramatic and prominent part of my secret world, but I was somehow entirely comfortable with it, which I found intriguing. These bodily experiences were quite dramatic, but I was somehow not immobilized or concerned. New experiences would

29

appear and become part of one integrated whole as I would assimilate everything together in one living odyssey that had become second nature to me. I reached a point that I didn't realize how abnormal I was. This was my life.

Because the unfolding of the Kundalini energy experiences had started to manifest toward the end of my tenure at the school, I never had the chance to speak to anyone about them, which left me, again, quite alone and confused. No one in my everyday life knew that I had any exposure to ideas related to energy or conscious evolution. This became a world I lived in by myself. I was continually caught off guard and flabbergasted by what felt like high-voltage electricity coursing through my nervous system. It was as though my body was generating and creating excessive energy, which then activated in my brain, expanding its bandwidth enough for me to encompass these uncanny physical experiences that I interpreted as the expansion of my consciousness. Without this sense of expansion, I don't think I could have gone through these experiences and faced the challenges and ups and downs of family and business life at the same time. It was becoming second nature for me to live this inner life of energy and conscious evolution while, simultaneously, I was commonplace and mundane to the people around me. I had created the perfect synergy for work on myself without the slightest utterance to anyone. I began recording these experiences in my notebooks in an effort to make sense of them. This was during the period I had begun to delve into the teachings of Jan Cox, whose ideas seemed to speak directly to my consciousness and my desire to expand in new and unpredictable directions. Only my wife, Nancy, knew that I was not very normal because she was aware of my strange habits, my odd physical manifestations, and my reading and studying things that seemed weird to her, to say the least. *Her greatest gift to me was that she never intervened.*

By this time, I was working in New York City, had two children, and was maintaining a rather high level of success that maintained our lifestyle while saving for the kids' college and our retirement. I did everything I could to keep my consciousness absorbed in The Work while I competently (to the best of my ability) tended to my responsibilities. Although the inner work grew, keeping up with it was sometimes harshly challenging. I had no external teacher at this time and wasn't attending classes, but I had learned the value of being a good householder. A good householder, as mentioned earlier, meant for me - living a sound life, maintaining a good marriage, and being the best father I could be. It was best described as having a healthy orientation in life. I also tried to do my job efficiently and be ready for the unexpected because adversity is inevitable. I was grateful for the life I lived and appreciated my health and family. I was also not without inspiration. I did my best and applied all the self-help psychology I'd studied earlier to help me along. To this end I would add that making a hobby out of manifesting a good healthy efficient life is rewarding on every level. Many of us unfortunately suffer from self-sabotage through self-hate. To hate one-self is largely universal—it is natural and easy but it is also existentially absurd. We must attack it by encompassing it like a helpless infant or an injured animal. We don't get angry at an injured animal, we compassionately try to help it because we understand it cannot help itself—a damaged ego and hurt personality is similar and we all have a higher intelligence that can help *if* we raise our consciousness enough to take on the challenge. One has to carefully disarm and diffuse a damaged ego like one would a bomb (the ego is very similar to a bomb).

The extraordinary thing was that through all of this, starting in my teens, I never felt *totally* alone. I *was* alone a lot, but I didn't *feel* alone. There is a big difference. The love I had for this inner calling, along with the addition of the wild electricity and energy running through my body, kept me focused, but what I was slowly beginning to realize was that, all along, I had *company*—company as in fellowship, friendship, and companionship.

This *company* is tricky to define and communicate because it is something that has been deeply private to me and something I never thought I would be putting into words for someone else to read, so bear with me. To fully appreciate the essence of *the company*, I have broken it up into three parts, but it is ultimately *one living experience*. Understand that what you are about to read unfolded in me over many years, so as you read through it, you may feel at times that you are getting it, then lose it, only to hopefully find it again—as I have. The first part of this idea involves a practical model of applied psychology; the second part will delve into the wonderful archetype of guides in literature, movies, and spirituality; and the third, and last part, explores how the extraordinary intelligence of nature and consciousness complete this one total phenomenon I am referring to as *the company*. Ultimately, it is all describing the idea of having a living field of creative energy accompany us on our journey through life—kind of like the feeling of togetherness between the Scarecrow, Tin Man, and Cowardly Lion as they joined Dorothy on her journey back home. This relationship bonds us to creation, which furnishes hope and possibly a higher state of interactive conscious evolution, and I realized that everyone has their own path and connection to it based on their unique individuality.

The Company and Diffusing the Hypnotism of Thought

The first essential part of what I am describing as "the company" begins with our inner consciousness and what we call the mind, or the thoughts that manifest in our head. Everyone would agree that we have thoughts, and when we are talking, these thoughts are the ones running through our mind as we verbalize. If we observe closely, there is also another part of us that is always listening to those thoughts and voices that talk in our heads; this is an inseparable part of us. Without it, we wouldn't be aware of ourselves. Most of us do not notice the sentient consciousness that is constantly *listening* to our mind. We switch back and forth between the talker and the listener so fast that we don't realize there appear to be two of us. This is an idea that Jan Cox elucidated for me in terms of describing the process as a tongue literally and suddenly turning into an ear—like one might envision in the surrealistic art of a Salvatore Dali painting (as Jan once said). Often, to comprehend new and higher states of consciousness, it is best to find art and music that take us to extraordinary places (most likely because the artists themselves were not in ordinary states of consciousness when inspired to create that particular work of art). We are not conscious of this arrangement naturally, yet it is profoundly transformational. I noticed a similar realization in Eckhart Tolle's account of his awakening when he explained reaching a point of mental suffering where he realized that he could not live with himself anymore. At that moment, he brilliantly asked himself who was the self he couldn't stand anymore and who was this mysterious self that was so bothered by the other. In other words, there would have to be two of him, *but he knew there could only be one*. Think about it. Can we *be* two beings at once? Are we not always that one being that is living and breathing but *have thoughts* that fool us into a dream world of thoughts, stories, and worries that keep us transfixed in a procession of ongoing, mostly contrived, possibilities and projections that are baseless and transitory? The question is whether we can create, feed, and empower the sentient awareness to a point of having a lasting focus on our inner mind and thoughts and thereby weaken their hold and become liberated from their mechanical control. To clearly understand this extraordinary idea, imagine, as you are reading this sentence, that suddenly an explosive blast of thunder shocked your attention out of the thought stream of reading this book, and you were suddenly just there—or here—in the now. You forget what you were reading, and your attention is now fully attuned to your surroundings in a survival mode. All thought vanishes, and you are, for a split second, enlightened. Meaning, there is no reverie of thought pulling you into your virtual thought world. There is just you breathing, peering, listening, and anticipating whether lightning is about to electrocute you through your roof or window … Then, two or three split seconds later, your attention shifts back into the stream of thought in yourself relative to the book (if you continue reading). If you are done reading, you go back to the stories in your head *about* your life (that is largely repetitive, neurotic, and self-created). We all need to be aware of the difference between dreaming in the mental narratives of the mind versus the brash experience of being hit over the head with a hammer and suddenly being awake in reality.

There is one other critical element to this practice that I want to touch relative to this psychological arrangement. It involves the movement of attention from the outside world to our inner world. What is most important for a person who has an inborn interest in conscious evolution is how bothered we are by the hypnotic hold of our own thoughts and how motivated we are to become liberated from such. Only then would such a separation begin to occur or have reason to fight and work against these thoughts. We need to ask ourselves *if* we are agitated by our own thoughts, stories, and mental narratives, or if we are content to live as we are. If content, we will not create new energy or find interest in working on ourselves (which is mostly the case and absolutely fine). For those who are either not content or downright outraged about their helpless condition relative to worry, fearful projections, and mental fabrications, there needs to be a disciplined connection to this process of differentiation or inner discernment. Like a connoisseur of wine, we must foster a conscious awareness of the quality, veracity, and profitability of the thoughts that appear in our minds. Those who have never simply watched the parade of thoughts in the mind *and checked them against reality* prepare your-self for the greatest circus on earth—prepare to want to cry and simultaneously laugh out loud.

In regard to how you personally *feel* toward these thoughts consider these three examples, which have all happened to me and most likely, in some variation on a theme, to you as well. Pay close attention not to the details of the example but more importantly to the level of intolerance to the thoughts that *feel* blind, senseless, and almost always incomplete and baseless.

Example 1:

The mind is worrying about the weather tomorrow, and we can hear the narratives surrounding that possibility ... (*how can this be,? why does this always happen to me? Life is against me ... only on my day off! I am disgusted ... life is awful*). This narrative is automatically playing like a repetitive reel on a tape, and we keep listening to it and getting bothered by it. It sounds like a parrot that has no consciousness of itself or its own repetitions. This inner newsfeed is boring and profitless. A higher state of consciousness realizes that we are better off making a phone call, rescheduling our plans, and enjoying the rainy day at home ... Ah, you know what? We can use a rainy day at home and now look forward to the new date, which calls for sun and blue skies.

The point of this example is becoming aware of how acting on superfluous thought and changing our plans liberates us from the disturbing mental chatter.

Example 2:

After receiving criticism about my physical appearance, I notice the mind bantering on with imaginary counterattacks, justifications, and explanations. One concocted defense after another spoken to an imaginary audience that is simply not there; it is all happening in my so-called mind. Who are these thoughts talking to? Why am I listening to them? How does the mind have such elaborate defenses always ready to react and defend?

What level of intelligence are such defenses? A higher consciousness decides: I am going to drive to the beach, jump in the cold water, swim in the waves, and annihilate these thoughts out of existence—not suppress them, because I hear them, understand them, and have watched them long enough. They bore me to tears ... All I feel now is the exciting cold water, the enjoyment of the blue sky, and the renewed energy of my body while in the water ... Criticism? I no longer hear anything!

The point again is taking physical action to annihilate the words that we otherwise cannot stop.

Example 3:

I remember the day I woke up and took a shower. When I was drying off, I looked in the mirror and saw a deep red welt across my midsection. It was not there yesterday, but it was about six inches long, beat red, and was beginning to burn. The mind immediately projected death, cancer, and severe suffering. The mind played out mental scenarios of telling my wife and kids I was dying and had six months to live ... I had a long day and many appointments and tried not to think about the red welt. Later, I got the chills and felt feverish. My mind was tormented by the imagination of what this all meant and how my life was suddenly ending. *How unfair! How absurd! How impossible that it is happening to me! Then again ... why not me?* More tragic thoughts played and sounded off in my mind as I hopelessly listened and suffered as a result. A small part of my consciousness was suspicious of all the neurosis but was no match for the torrent of terrifying thoughts. I then went to a skin doctor, and anticipating the word "cancer." He looked and immediately announced, "You have a case of the shingles, my friend."

As mentioned above, the importance of these examples is not the weather, a criticism, or a sudden physical symptom on or in the body. The point is that the inner, silent, sentient attention is listening, observing, and encompassing the thoughts *about* these situations and experiencing a growing contempt and repulsion toward their inaccurate and erroneous nature. In all three cases, I added *an action* that broke the spell of the thought pattern by changing the plan, jumping into cold water, and visiting a doctor to get the truth of my condition. It is this level of consciousness that longs for more reality and less frivolous thinking that we will focus on, expand, and follow to a potentially new state of being. This elusive intelligence is in all of us, quietly waiting for new fun to begin. It is bored with the same old predictable reactions that play like a broken record. It longs for a guide to lead it out of this condition it finds itself in. Are you bored with your mind and the way it relates to your life? In my case, this leads to what I am calling a guide, but everyone can have a different experience of finding their way out of the labyrinth of their mind.

The important thing to realize at this point is that there just might be a higher-evolved intelligence in all of us, *if* we can learn to talk less and listen more. This is why meditation is very compelling and fulfilling. The unspeaking higher intelligence in the brain is given space to be, to listen, to experience this other state and work toward building a higher quality of attention, so we don't identify with every thought that appears in the mind. This is why we often value quiet time or what some people call "me time," which can be quite healthy. This part of our brain is also supremely rational, reasonable, and logical, which it derives from a masterful source that brings us to the second part of the *company*. Keep in mind that this silent, inner awareness of our being will seek more of itself and shun what is unreal, illogical, contrived, and made up. Consider also that this extraordinary part of our being does not reject *all* thought (although it comes close), but favors thoughts that are aligned with its own nature. It gravitates toward thoughts that are accurate, creative, growth oriented, compassionate, and empathetic—all the characteristics that humanity has recognized as good, saintly, fair, and profitable to the species.

Starting from this wordless level of consciousness, I will explain the next critical part of what I mean by having *company* along the way on this journey. Imagine that we all have a highly intelligent being or entity present in our heads that accompanies us through our lives. This idea is a very powerful universal idea that has inspired individual people for centuries and remains today as a beautiful and uplifting theme that resonates in all of us. From my perspective, this theme is no accident and has a quite astonishing source that is closer to us than we think. Consider these three examples from literature, fantasy, and spirituality in terms of a guide. Notice the compelling power and timeless appeal of this theme and consider how it has impacted billions of people by inspiring hope and growth:

In Literature: *The Divine Comedy* is a classic work of literature that has been argued as one of the greatest books of all time, an Italian masterpiece written by the poet Dante Alighieri and completed in the year 1320. In this book, the main character and writer, Dante, finds himself "lost in a dark wood," which allegorically means that he has lost his way; he isn't sure where to go in life and is seeking answers—*like most of us*. While being lost, he's confronted with the challenges of his inner nature and longs to find salvation and liberation, which for him would be found in God. What is pertinent from my perspective is the arrival of guides. In *The Divine Comedy*, two guides arrive to aid Dante on his journey. The first guide is Virgil, who represents reason and rationality, and the second guide is Beatrice, who represents the supreme intelligence that transcends logic and reason in the form of divine love. These guides represent a higher form of intelligence and guidance that we all long for and wish we had available to us, *which is where I am going*. Notice that help arrives first as pure rationality and logic to help him find his way, but at a certain point in his journey, reason and rationality must be left behind and handed to a level of intelligence that is beyond thought and logic. This leap from rationality to the mystical and unknowable is a powerful theme of the human spirit, as we shall see.

In Fantasy: In two of the most successful epics in movie-making history, *Lord of the Rings* and *Star Wars*, there is the same universal theme of guidance, help, and the realm of supernatural intelligence. In *Lord of the Rings*, which is based on the book by J. R. R. Tolkien (1892–1973), the main character, Frodo Baggins, takes on an extraordinary journey of his own to rid the world of a ring that has inconceivable power, which, in the wrong hands, can wreak havoc and evil on the world (much like our egos). Throughout the journey, higher intelligence accompanies him in different forms but most prominently through a wizard named Gandalf, who is his companion, friend, and, most importantly, his guide through the challenges of his journey. Gandalf, like Virgil to Dante, provides a companion of reason and rationality to help guide and direct. Ultimately, Frodo learns to rely on his own intuitive understanding to reach his destiny, often by using powers that exceed reason and rationality. In *Star Wars*, it is the powerful concept of *The Force* that represents the higher intelligence of the universe, which communicates directly to the Jedi who *has transformed himself* to align with The Force. As a consequence of that alignment (which takes work on oneself), the Force comes to the aid of the Jedi in the form of a teacher like Yoda, and ultimately, like Frodo, in the realm of his own being. The universal theme of a guide or some form of help to the aspiring seeker is one of the themes in the movie series that is so moving and energizing to the vast audiences these films attract. We must all *feel* in ourselves this restless energy that longs to connect to a higher power. The deeper question is whether we have a source within us that we personally can connect to that helps us through our journey in life.

In Spirituality: Circa 2017, we find religion spiraling quickly away from the young generations as it becomes increasingly incredulous, preposterous, and under severe attacks from the growing number of atheists, backed by science and sheer anger at how provincial and non-inclusive religion is in the broad spectrum of human experience. While this is factual and clearly a change in the course of humanity, people need to be careful not to debunk the essence of the teachings that underlie the major religions. We have to differentiate between the dogmas created by ordinary people versus the pure teachings that were transmitted by highly evolved beings. In the essence of these teachings that maintain universal appeal, the entire concept of help from the outside is what drives a spiritual journey. We seek guidance, and we look to some higher incarnation of being and intelligence to help and guide us. People pray, people surrender to a higher power, and people feel more secure believing that a higher force of intelligence is ultimately behind all of creation. In Christianity, there is the Holy Spirit, and in the Yoga Sutras of Patanjali, there is Icvara, which both represent the concept of a living force outside of time that has intelligence and is responsive to seekers. In short, reciprocal energy engages beings who seek help and responds by giving seekers the extraordinary experience of being engaged in life and their own personal growth and evolution. Many people today are losing this invaluable connection to any higher source of intelligence and have become hypnotically self-absorbed through the technology that invariably feeds the blog of themselves.

The refined and distilled question is whether there actually is a truly powerful source of intelligence that would serve as what I am referring to as *"company"* along the journey toward higher experience. Are all such involvements in imaginary guides, divine intervention, wizards, angels, and idyllic concepts like the Force without merit? Am I, too, about to depart from reason and rationality, leaving science and logic, to also explore some fanciful and imaginary fiction that my reader may find loathsome and pathetic? Am I going to speak in terms similar to worshipping the tooth fairy, Santa, or the Easter bunny? I can only say at this point that I do have and have had company on my journey, and I hope you agree by the end of this section that this "imaginary" friend is quite real, absurdly powerful, and virtually magical—and *needs* us all to grow without limits.

In order to explain the third and final part of this living phenomenon and relationship I call *the company*, here's a story that goes back to my college days. Remember to remain open-minded, and I will tie it all together later on:

When I was an undergraduate at Fordham University (I transferred from a 2 year Community College to Fordham University in 1982), I majored in psychology and took a class called Creativity. The content of the class was to explore the nature and history of the phenomenon of creativity, but the class focused largely on human creativity by exploring its many forms—writing, music, art, architecture, innovation. The course required us to write a final paper on a topic of our choice, and I decided not to write a paper on human *creativity but instead on the creativity exemplified by life in nature.* In short, the paper was about problem-solving, the ways that nature, not humans, solves problems. Simply put, challenges, like staying safe, capturing food, and moving from one place to another, can all be understood as problem-solving—by nature. I was always startled not only by the ingenuity of nature and how wonderfully creative its solutions are but also by the fact that it could generate out of itself precisely the chemical and physical apparatus needed to solve an almost impossible challenge. I found this reality to be as creative as the solution itself. Two examples have stayed with me since I wrote the original paper, and a third I have since added. Keep in mind that these examples are meant to be understood within a specific context to make an intentional point relative to conscious evolution and Kundalini energy. They aren't meant to point to something obvious. Pay attention to your feelings and sensations as you read through these in addition to the actual content. This is not the actual paper but a paraphrase:

Rich Mollura

Life and Flight

Looking out at nature, it is easy *not* to be astonished at how outlandish it is that *life flies*. As infants, we are surrounded by birds and insects as well as airplanes and helicopters. Children and adults alike may feel a sense of awe and wonder about flight for a few fleeting seconds but soon after absorb this extraordinariness into their everyday awareness of life and not give it another thought. Yet consider what happened. At some point, life, that had not been able to fly, started flying! The idea alone is shocking. Flight was not a given. The concept of flight did not exist in any form *before it started happening.* Matter and cells *never flew before.* Think about the first creature that ever flew on this earth. How did it grow wings that would have had little to no purpose until they could actually use them to fly? How did the wings evolve so perfectly for such a complex phenomenon? How was there the right muscle strength to move the wings to keep them going? How did this creature have the bioenergy to maintain flight? How did it know where to go and not perish while trying to get somewhere when it had never flown before? Flight was a creative solution to the problem of ensuring survival—but what an extraordinary solution! How uncanny is the fact that life bore out of itself all the highly refined physical features, the ultracomplex engineering, and the earth navigation (which it had never encountered from the air before)?

Simply look at a caterpillar. Would you ever think it would someday fly in the form of a butterfly, of all things? The cocoon itself would have taken millions of years to evolve, but would it have had any use at all without the blueprint of transforming into a butterfly? A caterpillar crawling on a tree ends up flying from California to Mexico, where there is warmer weather and it has a greater chance of survival. Quite impressive and profound. And I am not making this point to argue about evolution or creationism. Science theorizes that there are answers to all these questions, given the prodigious amount of time creatures have been evolving and the theory of natural selection, but that is not our concern, as we will see. I am making this point with a highly specific idea in mind—about the creativity and extraordinary breadth of that creativity and manifestation (no matter how it happened)—and *we are* that same creative source yet with the addition of consciousness.

Life and the Orb Web of a Spider

Quite a long time ago, I was taking a walk in nature and came upon a fully formed and completed orb web of a spider. My attention was gripped by this rather eccentric solution to yet another challenge for life relative to growth and survival. Again, what an unconventional and creative idea! The spider needs to eat flying insects and yet does not fly like a bird or have a long, sticky tongue like a frog or lizard to catch food (another astonishing design). Basically, the logic is to weave a virtually invisible web that it somehow knows the flying insects can't see, trap the insect within the stickiness of the web, then eat it. But even more intriguing and compelling to me was the evolution of the chemical substance of the silk that the spider uses to form the web. I remember thinking, *Wouldn't there have to have been the design of the web and the finished idea of how it would work before it could evolve such a perfect substance as silk?* Today, we still marvel at this extraordinary substance. And what about the physical mechanism it would need to store, release, and coordinate the expulsion of the silk? The silk of the spider has a flawless constitution for its purpose, and many spiders use multiple silks to complete their webs. It is quite an improbable chemical and physical complexity for such an awesome manifestation and successful design. Lastly, how does the spider know where to start the web and how to navigate the periphery around bushes and trees that it cannot see from a distance? I can go on, but again, I have a certain point in mind, and it is not to educate readers on spider webs or flight.

Consciousness

Consciousness is the third example, the one I added to flight and the orb web of the spider since my college paper. Of all the fantastic and endless creations of life through nature, nothing compares to the creation of consciousness. I am writing this book with consciousness, and you are reading the words I have written with consciousness, and neither one of us has any idea what consciousness is! What is the bioelectrochemical makeup of this invisible substance we refer to when we say, "I am conscious"? Just the idea that this "substance" was *created* should blow our minds. Consciousness

41

itself had to be created—unless it has always existed—which is even more profound. How—and better yet, why—would consciousness evolve the way it did? Life thrived on this planet for billions of years before human consciousness came into being. Billions of years is a very long time. Think about it! (thinking about it for yourself is the ultimate key of this entire book). If we are not awed, stunned, and grateful all at the same time, then it is unlikely that we will have the spirit to grow and evolve into a new level of consciousness. Consider that this is exactly what life wants and needs. Life certainly has the means and aptitude to create consciousness, but as far as we can tell, we are the first time life uses conscious beings to participate in her magnificent creation. We should be tickled and quite excited. When we *understand* this single inviting fact, we feel much less alone (existentionally).

If we feel a sense of awe and wonder sharing these revelations and observations and we can appreciate the clear biological genius of nature, consider the fact that *we*, our bodies and the consciousness that constitutes our identity, are inseparable from—and *are*—that very same living and very much alive creative and intelligent energy. In other words, all of humanity, in a very real and literal sense, embodies all of the spectacularly successful biological blueprints of nature in its very gene pool. This is what makes human creativity and human potential so unimaginably infinite and also could account for a lot of the supernatural phenomena we see permeating our history. This is a very important idea that deserves a few quick examples to clarify. I will try to make them short and limit them to three because I can go on forever in this direction. I am not seeking to prove these ideas but only suggest *possibilities* that can be profitable to human growth and self-propelled evolution. If you find yourself trying to argue against them and prove them wrong, then enjoy the process of thinking but don't imagine I would debate you (unless for fun). These three examples exemplify how the masterful creation of life may be inseparably embroidered within human creativity and evolution and stir a sense of the miraculous:

Life Accesses Its Ingenious Designs and Explodes through Human Consciousness

Early civilizations have boggled our minds with uncanny and almost supernormal feats of intelligent design in architecture, science, and art. Can it be that life has biologically arranged that human consciousness is indirectly accessing the very repository of blueprints of its own ancient lineage of highly successful creation? In other words, when human beings started to navigate the earth and skies, was the knowledge of earth navigation, which was already highly refined in the genetic code of insects and birds, indirectly accessed? I was always curious about how the design of the flight of a helicopter was ominously similar to the flight of a bee. Could it be that the very design of the flight of a bee was sublimely interfused in the design of a helicopter? That the human consciousness of certain individuals experienced literal and direct access to the successfully evolved blueprints of flight in general, and the helicopter in particular, and that other human beings, encoded and pervaded with the same genetic material, added to the original ideas that led to all modes of flight for humans? This, of course, would not be a direct process; the newly evolved human consciousness would be receiving hints, fragments, and suggestions in the form of ideas that needed to be fleshed out through trial and error, which accounts for the history of all inventions. Is it not fascinating and almost eerie how humanity invented the lightbulb but that there are such things in nature as lightning, lightning bugs, and electric eels? Can you think of or see any of these reflections of nature in human innovation? Thus, the brilliance of human ingenuity may be accessing the very storehouse of design and experience of life itself. The examples are endless. It compels one to rethink how humanity built pyramids, evolved complex civilizations, and conjured up such a variety of governing systems, just to mention a few. Life has done all this before, and quite well, just never through consciousness.

Human Prodigy—Life's Ancient, Masterful Intelligence Repurposes Itself in Individuals

Consider the mystery of the prodigy phenomenon that runs inarguably through humanity. It is very difficult to account for unlearned and freakish manifestations of talent we see in highly gifted children. It could be mathematical, scientific, artistic, or even physical capabilities that go beyond logic. Many of these gifted children have not had time to externally learn these amazing gifts, yet they have them. This all becomes quite possible if we consider that humanity has indirect, although literal and precise, access to the very same brilliance of nature and the endless number of successfully engineered designs that preceded us. The child also does not have to be a so-called prodigy; all humans have a range of talent, and some are more advanced than others in specific fields. This could also account for how certain human beings can be considered handicapped in some areas and a genius in others. What if the collective gene pool of life gets activated in different people and even at different stages of their life? This may sound like I am saying it is all genetics, but it is the context of this possibility that will make the difference. Genetics and instinct deserve a much deeper dive. Again, consider examples for yourself. Look around, think, and imagine such possibilities. Peer at human genius and ponder whether it is nature, as if in disguise, using tested designs but using human intelligence to expand, reach, and explore brand-new terrain and horizons—brains into computers? Consider again the idea referenced earlier that life is alive and growing through everything, and it has a dazzling array of successful designs to access and play with relative to all future creation and evolution.

Human Wisdom, Mystical Beings, and Enlightenment— Life's Distilled Precision and Magnificence

The third connection to consider relative to this idea of accessing the creative brilliance of life through human consciousness involves the teachings that emanate from mystics, esoteric teachers, and the so-called enlightened. These rare and unusual teachings reflect the highest level of human potential relative to inner being and serve as an elusive yet magnetic ideal toward which collective humanity strives. While these teachings are at the center of all the major religions of the world, they are certainly not limited to them, and their merit can be found in many different mediums. It is important that we suspend all automatic judgment of the most traditional teachings and consider the phenomenon of higher wisdom from a different vantage point—*that life itself embodies an extraordinary storehouse of higher understanding that it needs to incarnate consciously through humanity*; that more than anything else, life itself needs to grow and flourish into its next generation of creation. It may be noted that I may be alluding to or hinting toward a conception of God, without using the term, but I leave that up to the reader to decide what *they think*. I personally am against any childish dependence on any word that might blunt one's own active participation in the process of evolving one's own consciousness. That said, I personally think the word God is the most powerful word in the human language and resonates the energy the word imparts to us.

Just as my attention was absorbed and engrossed by the phenomena of flight, spider webs, and prodigies, I became equally curious about how exquisitely preconceived and strikingly comprehensive spiritual teachings are. They all have an unusual constitution and confounding preeminence. We have to consider the incontestable and irrefutable fact that these systems of teaching have an unworldly yet timeless appeal that is also strangely authoritative. How does such a fully elaborate and finely connected system of ideas form in a human brain? How does it find an expression that communicates its message with supernormal effectiveness as in parables and sutras? And how does it then last thousands of years and help empower conscious evolution through centuries of inconceivable upheaval and change? The skeptics usually debunk such teachings by focusing on the non-thinking interpretations of the masses and the absurd atrocities carried out by religious zealots. This type of logic, if applied to science, would be like discarding science because of pollution and nuclear warheads. We need to pay attention to and focus on the actual nectar of the teachings themselves and ask ourselves how such teachings could have possibly generated themselves before their utterance or what they are in the context of evolution. There is a profound mystery not only in the teachings themselves but also in how they flow and spontaneously intersperse into collective human consciousness. I need to be sure I stay on point and emphasize that I am focusing specifically on the rarely considered *nonverbal* source of the origin of such ideas and hope to increase our appreciation of a most extraordinary phenomenon. Could life have found its own joy in creating new ways to unleash its creative genius through human consciousness? Does the genius of nature speak clearly and powerfully through these teachings? Consider the simple wisdom from the Native American Indians in how close to nature they were, how they exuded a peaceful kinship with the earth, and how life always served as a mentor and not an enemy. Connect the teachings of Zen with Native American Indians and then reflect on the wisdom of yoga or the teachings of Jesus. Read the four excerpts below and see if you sense how these teachings speak a particular higher language and transmit different energy than ordinary information:

> Religion is for people afraid to go to hell; Spirituality is for those who have been there.
>
> —Vine Deloria, Sioux (Native American wisdom)

> You will not be punished for your anger; you will be punished by your anger.
>
> —Buddha

> Yoga is the practice of tolerating the consequences of being yourself.
> —Bhagavad Gita

> He who is without sin cast the first stone.
> —Jesus

These are universal teachings that speak directly to the higher places in oneself, built into the very fabric of our being. When these teachings are rightly received, it is as though we are recognizing reality and truth, rather than taking in information we have to process and memorize. Ask yourself what you think about relative to the above quotations and points. Consider the practice of pondering wisdom and nature as one source of comfort and companionship. Nature's spectacular ingenuity and human wisdom are one and the same, like music can flow from a violin, a piano, or a bass drum. It is all music, and it is all within us.

Circling back to the company on the journey and connecting it to the spectacular literal capabilities of life, I will begin to tie all this together in the way it makes sense to me (currently). The point I am making is that the company I referenced earlier is this very same inconceivable wisdom of life itself. That same source of unbounded intelligence and creativity is now activating higher energies in the body, interconnecting new ways of processing our existence, and forming the future evolution of the collective consciousness of all of humanity. It is critical that we recognize this extraordinary presence of intelligence in ourselves and develop a benevolent and mutually coefficient relationship to that unfathomable source of energy and creativity. Keep in mind, again, the fact that life not only authors exquisitely imaginative and innovative solutions to challenges but also manufactures, *out of itself*, precise biology specific to that end. It is in this light that we must revisit what Kundalini energy might be, as well as the details of conscious evolution.

Stated simply, it is quite possible, from a literal and biological point of view, that life's massive capabilities are behind all human potential, and everything that is good in humanity is a testament to this reality. The challenge is to maintain this perspective while being bound to the habitual patterns of our hardwired ego, personality, and mind. Equally challenging is that the level of humanity that rules the external world through government and politics reflects the maturity of our place in evolution as well. Both the individual level of consciousness and the collective level of consciousness of humanity are young, compulsive, and driven by power and violence (which is our current evolutionary status). The individual and humanity as a collective race are on their own paths of growth and evolution, and each takes time and work. The focus of this book is the individual. Growth on the collective scale operates over centuries and millennium and mixes with the evolution of the individual in a unique and complex way. The growth of our collective evolution is beyond the scope of this book. The growth of higher consciousness within an individual is complex and varies greatly. A person can truly cherish the idea of living a more liberated and consciously centered life and continually find him or herself in states so completely opposite that it is disillusioning and disheartening. In addition, the external world of events delivers a stream of bad news in the form of human hostility, random accidents, and dreadful illness that makes life feel hopelessly cynical (which are life's greatest challenges that often entrap most of us). It is for this reason that some teachers called this inner journey *work*. To work on one's self requires relentless effort to transcend the mechanical sense of self. No matter how many times we fall off the horse, we must press on and get back on (we must always consider the alternative, which is to fall victim and suffer terribly). To those people who have the deepest calling to work on themselves, there is no choice. This is an important point relative to the science of seeking higher understanding and being. Each person is born to a different level or need to alter their own being and consciousness. Most people have zero interest in any of the ideas I am talking about and find it completely foreign and absolutely unnecessary to live a good life (and they are right—for themselves). Other people encompass a range of interests from enjoying information like this as a weekend hobby to those who try hard to engage in change with varying degrees of success. There are also a group of people who can't stop working on it to their very last breath. I can't account for how and why this is so. I only know that it is absolutely the case—as I am an example of this—and we must all seek our own level of fulfillment, whatever that might be. We should also consider the idea I mentioned earlier in the book, that humanity is a very young race that is most likely growing out of its infancy and *hopefully* will make it to adolescence and beyond. It is our responsibility to swallow the bitter pill that life will appear utterly heartless and impersonal in times of tragedy and calamity. In the moment, such things are impossible for our current level of consciousness to comprehend, yet, strangely, we move forward and get through the most tragic of realities.

As for The Work as I understand it today, I believe it is of dire importance to nurture first a deep respect and reverence to life itself and then nourish this kinship with life. It need not be through spiders, caterpillars, and butterflies. It could be through helping other people, caring for animals, or virtually anything that makes a person feel good. It could be through music, art, and dance—or from how we conduct ourselves relative to others and how we do our absolute best to understand other people's perspectives (no matter how different from our own). The point is that self-actualization comes from a person's unique core, and if developed properly, it flourishes and becomes part of one's life purpose. Once a person is grounded in life and feels a sense of being at home within their existence, it is essential to pay close attention to the physical energy of life and do what we can, given our genetic disposition, to align the body for maximum generation of energy. This means working on all four levels of being—body, emotion, mind, and consciousness/spirituality. In the next section of this book, in which I outline the full unleashing of what I refer to as my Kundalini experience, it may be noted that these experiences started out as physical, transitioned to emotional, then intellectual, and then cohesively interconnected into a form of higher consciousness and spirituality. I conceive of spirituality as the collective result of a lifetime of nurturing the highest levels of oneself relative to energy, consciousness, and respect and gratitude toward life. As mentioned above, to live in awe, for me, is to be spiritual, and one can be a spiritual religious person or a spiritual atheist from my perspective. That is a personal decision (that is, if you dare to live in the brutal world of labeling your-self as anything).

As we move our discussion toward the higher level of ourselves, it is critical that we address the idea of optimizing the quality and quantity of the energy that *we* produce. I personally advocate a middle-of-the-road approach and feel that any extremism wastes more energy than it creates. Our bodies are subject to illness, aging, and eventual passing, no matter what we eat, drink, or do, and that must be remembered so we do not become fanatical and unrealistic. We are also subject to accidents that can suddenly alter our fate and destiny. This should be remembered to keep us humble throughout our lives and keep things in perspective. Whether we become movie stars, achieve great accomplishments, or earn millions if not billions of dollars, we all meet the exact same fate. Eliminating obvious toxins, engaging in movement and exercise of some form or other, eating reasonably well, breathing correctly, and aligning the body often all contribute to good health, but more importantly, *it creates more energy.* This same approach can be considered regarding emotion and mind. Negative emotions,—like fear, sadness, and hostility burn excessive energy; as do thoughts that are pessimistic, critical, angry, and judgmental. We cannot deny our nature, but we can learn to understand, accept, and transcend it. There are numerous books and opportunities to help us become more balanced human beings, but I want to focus on higher energies and conscious evolution as we continue this exploration. The stark and astonishing question is whether life itself embodies and operates with an intelligence and source of energy that is truly beyond and outside the normal range of our everyday thinking. Are supernatural energies driving our very existence and moving toward a higher target of evolution? If so, then it is possible and expected that this extraordinary reality would appear in everyday life. Where else could it? From my perspective, it is everywhere, but our minds are so conditioned to accept only a certain range of experience that we have been exposed to that we generally do not accept extreme variations from others. This is what draws us to freak shows, outlandish displays of talent, and great art in all of its forms. I know without a shadow of a doubt that if I read about the following Kundalini energy experiences prior to my experience, I would be suspicious and question it on many fronts, *but biology does not lie.* What is *is,* and any rejection of *any* manifestation of life is a grave mistake and an irrefutable example of limited consciousness. I have always been curious as to why and how we can accept the horrifying potentials of malady and disease of the body but are not filled with awe when our bodies deliver outstanding physical feats, breaking all sorts of uncanny records and delivering mind-dazzling masterpieces of creativity that defy logic, whether through music, poetry, literature, technology, or dance. I will open up to the full detail of my experience in the following section and conclude by tying it together with my current speculations and ruminations relative to what this offers us and what value this book might bring to those attracted to it. I would also like to prepare my reader by saying that some of the descriptions demand that I pull ideas from other teachers and writers and use concepts most likely never heard before, or certainly not pulled together in this particular context. My goal is certainly not to espouse the full teachings of those who influenced and impacted me but to urge without question any and all follow-up to their work available to the public through their websites, books, and talks.

SECTION III

Kundalini—Explosive, Intelligent, and Endearing

I have alluded to the Kundalini experiences but so far have not delivered the full details. As mentioned earlier, this book began as an account of this extraordinary topic, but the further I delved, the more I realized it would be impossible to write about Kundalini without the context of my personal calling and search for the answer to that question I posed as a teenager: *where does life ultimately lead?* I realized I could not write about Kundalini without writing about conscious evolution; they were one and the same thing. The key to understanding what I mean by conscious evolution and Kundalini energy lies in the extraordinary nature of creativity in that *creativity requires both energy and intelligence combined.* Just like a rocket or a high-performance sports car like a Ferrari requires a high-octane fuel, so does work on our self-evolution. It is my contention that the human body is equipped with a physiology that can generate profoundly new experiences as it evolves into its future. The strange thing is that it should not come as a surprise. As we have seen, nature displays endless wonders effortlessly, so why would nature not offer new and unexplored territory in her most innovative creation—the human being? I believe the issue is not whether this is the case but whether we are simply looking at what humanity has been doing and *is* doing right now before our eyes, with this notion in mind. This is precisely why I addressed the miracles of nature and how that same ingenious intelligence has manifested as the wonders of ancient civilizations, progenies, and geniuses, and how it has delivered profound wisdom through mystics and avatars. It is endless when our eyes are wide open. In this section, I will detail a phenomenon that I am as curious and unsure about as you might be. It is important that we keep our consciousness energized, alert, and open to all possibilities and maintain an explorative spirit while we share the following experiences and manifestations—not only in my life but in all our lives. I do want to add, up front and before we journey into more detail, that while it may sound like one *needs* to have an activated Kundalini to pursue higher states of consciousness, it is more mysterious than even that. Many of the most renowned spiritual teachers made no mention of such unusual manifestations (some did but chose not to discuss it). Thus, unusual physical manifestations *are not* a prerequisite to pursuing higher states of consciousness. I am also not saying that since these experiences have been highly active in me that I am somehow a teacher of higher consciousness, because I am clearly not. My fate did not lead anywhere close to one who attracts students and spends their life teaching others. While I maintain that this higher energy is underlying all creativity, and most especially through great spiritual teachers, it can, and mostly does, manifest *through the teaching itself* without ever manifesting outward or physically. This all contributes to one of the most compelling realities of this entire field of esoteric evolution: *never assume or expect human logic to explain life's bewildering creation; it is beyond everything that our current level of intelligence can ever know or understand.*

Kundalini refers to the physical energy of transformation and creation that powers the superior intelligence of evolution through humanity. As mentioned above, it is ultimately the source of all creativity but becomes more specific through humanity as evolution propels itself. From this perspective, we should buckle our seat belts and get ready for new human phenomena that might break our conditioned expectations and re-envision or re-imagine what humanity can become. Putting the question in simple terms, if evolution can produce flight, silk, and consciousness (just to name a few), what can it do through the evolving matter and consciousness that stems *from that exact same source?* Again, we are joining a party that has been surviving and evolving for more than four billion years. It is important to realize that nature, consciousness, and Kundalini are all one phenomenon and is exploding through our branch of evolution *now*. Many of us assume that evolution has stopped, but why do we make such an absurd claim?

Most of us do not see, feel, and remember that life has been surging and ever growing for a very long time, and we are part of that lineage. Life is a living and growing process, and, as I quoted Jan Cox earlier, "Life itself is Alive." I have found it helpful to use the analogy that our minds, due to their level of consciousness, experience life as one frame of an epic film during a single lifetime. In other words, if we looked and lived within a single frame of a movie, would it or could it make sense? Everything must be seen as growing from one stage into another. To look at a tadpole and then look at a frog, at two separate moments, without observing the transformation that takes place, who would think it is the exact same creature? Similarly, life is always growing and transforming on this planet. It is a work forever in transition, and to dissect it, without factoring in motion, would kill it.

Kundalini Experiences in Full Detail

Keeping in mind this notion that life is transforming, I want to circle back to that moment back in time when I had my first Kundalini energy experience. What followed from that initial bioelectrical shock that shot through my body led to additional experiences that unfolded over time. The physical experiences were inseparably integrated with the intellectual search, and thus, ultimately, I see them as one unified internal experience. While it is true that my quest for a new state of consciousness preceded these physical manifestations chronologically, I now understand that the two were always one comprehensive and interconnected experience (as everything has to be). As will come to light, all the experiences derive first from the body (or the energy of the body) and then expand into the emotions, mind, and consciousness. How could any experience start anywhere other than with the energy and matter of our living body? The most profound reality for me was that the entire experience embodied an interconnected intelligence that revealed itself over time.

A few important points about what follows: First, everything I speak of is *biology*, which is why I spoke earlier of flight, the silk of spiders, and consciousness as organic creations. Life does, can, and will create new biology through evolution, and not by waving a magic wand but gradually, over very long periods of time with periodioc hyper-bursts of creative leaps.

Everything we see around us had to have changed slowly over time to become what it is now. *How* all this happens, I cannot say and is not within the scope of this book. I will say that every time I thought we had it all figured out, we didn't. Everything is infinitely mysterious.

Secondly, while I am calling this experience a Kundalini experience, I am doing so because it's the best historical reference I have found. Kundalini energy has never been measured or actually observed directly because science has not yet devised the technology to identify, measure, or study it. I have struggled with this fact and have been mentally taunted by whether this is an energy, a neurophysiological aberration, or both. I have also struggled with the idea of whether this is actual evolution in formation. It certainly *feels like* an overpowering electrical unleashing of energy that has an inconceivable intelligence of its own. I remain open to all possibilities, but of one thing I am absolutely sure: *my biology has changed in my lifetime and what you are about to read is a direct account after thirty-five years of it's unfolding.* Thirdly, although some of the descriptions will sound familiar to people who have had similar experiences or who have read books about the subject, many may sound unconventional and not follow fundamental and classic reports or models of Kundalini. I have resolved to communicate what I have experienced without trying to make it fit into any previously documented accounts. At the same time, there have been many recorded experiences of Kundalini that I personally have not had. This reality that Kundalini manifestations are limitless and creative beyond our imagination is a very good thing. Who wants anything to be predictable? Predictable is boring, especially when speaking of our existence.

Lastly, while I have enumerated more than ninety such manifestations in my personal logs, I have since refined them into the physical experiences and then the transformative impact on the totality of my being. I have consolidated, condensed, and aligned these descriptions in a way that limits repetition. Many will sound almost mundane and questionable, and you may wonder whether that particular experience has anything to do with Kundalini. But I am writing about how these experiences align and connect as one totality that makes up what I refer to as the Kundalini experience *within me.* Keep in mind that one of Kundalini's most profound mysteries is that it can manifest uniquely in different people; that is the nature of its genius. It is creative, eccentric, and dynamic. It can also manifest through one or multiple mediums (like music, art, or dance) and does not need to express itself in any one way, which I mentioned above. This energy is almost like having a naturally produced recreational drug released directly into one's blood, brain, and nervous system - which, with an aligned perspective, could deliver unspeakable joy and excitement that is healthy for the human spirit. From my view, it is the enlivening and underlying energy that drives everything that is creative and enjoyable. We must keep in mind, however, that the energy has profound potential, and only our conditioned thinking imposes limits that constrain it. I would add that while this energy can and does permeate all creativity and change, there is a distinct difference when it becomes an activated biophysiological process in our body. What I mean is that, just as the body undergoes a drastic change from a fetus to an infant or a child to an adolescent, *the literal physiology is changing*. It is not theoretical, and therefore this is not dreamy, flowery mysticism. These experiences are as real as when teeth first start breaking the gums of an infant or facial hair starts emerging from the skin of an adolescent. The difference, of course, is that direct Kundalini experience is not a preprogrammed, automatic phenomenon, as opposed to the former examples. This is largely what accounts for its mystery. I am going to break this down in detail by explaining exactly what happened in my body over the years from the release of this powerful energy. If you are a reader who has had Kundalini experiences or has studied Kundalini, you will find some familiar manifestations. On the other hand, if this is all new, then keep an open mind and ask yourself if you have experienced any variations of these accounts; also remember that hundreds of books have been written about Kundalini, so it is not all new. In regard to whether you can relate to what follows, I am sure you will be able to identify with some, but consider again, as mentioned earlier, that if you have experimented with psychedelic drugs, have experienced the sheer force of sexual energy, have laughed hysterically and uncontrollably, or have been overwhelmed with ecstatic joy relative to a creative act or a feeling of pure love, then this energy was activated on some level. It all hails from the magical source of nature that is already in us.

Of all the physical Kundalini experiences I've had, there are fifteen I'll talk about. I hope these descriptions open a door for you to foster your own growth and view them from the perspective that they are not just my experiences. I see them as *life's* experiences, which there are many variations of. After I discuss these specific experiences, I'll move on to talk about the elaborate integration of the higher centers of emotion, mind, and consciousness that are the hidden gifts inside these physical experiences. What I mean by integration is that whatever this emerging mode of human experience is, its chief highlight is that it does not simply end in one new place but seeks to reach across the entirety of our being. Just like a fertilized egg has an innate drive to become a fully grown being, this experience appears to have its own trajectory toward a completed state. Like the drive of humanity to explore just about everything, so does the intelligence of this experience seek to forever traverse new territory, which includes our emotions, mind, and consciousness. It is the spirit of creative introspection that I hope to ignite a life-long, ever growing and expanding venture to connect more of this ingenious life together.

As you read through these fifteen physical manifestations, keep one very important observation in mind: our bodies are *always* doing things *before* our awareness of them. Consider the classic yawn in which a person's body stretches and reaches out as it yawns. The body starts to stretch, yawn, and moan—*and then* we make a comment like "I'm tired." This is important because the body is adjusting to some inner condition without our pre-awareness. Life and our bodies are way ahead of our thoughts. I've been tracking and tracing these manifestations for many years. The best way I can encapsulate what you are about to read is to say that the highest levels of creative energy have an innate course of action in our body, no different from puberty or menopause, that enacts preordained physical transformations of the body so that this energy can flow and transform us over time. To be clear, I will deliver these physical experiences in detail before exploring the emotional, intellectual, and spiritual impact of the overall experience.

The Physical Manifestations of Kundalini and the Body's need to accommodate New and Powerful Kundalini Activity

1. Bioelectrical Shocks

Electricity is a highly distinct and unmistakable phenomenon. When we think of electricity, we think of lightning or the unmistakable sensation of touching a live electrical socket with our finger. We feel a current that causes a sudden jolt that instantaneously throws the body into an immediate reflex away from the source. As I mentioned previously, the first unusual bodily experience I had was an electrical shock that triggered suddenly and ran a specific route through my body and down my arm. That experience, over the course of thirty-five years, not only did not wane or cease but continued to move progressively through most of the areas of my body with greater frequency and increasing intensity. It is important to note that while they were somewhat involuntary jolts of energy when they first happened, they were almost immediately under my conscious control. What I mean by this is that there is a subtle moment of a buildup (similar to a pre-orgasm ramp up) during which I am aware that a shock is about to happen. In that split second, I have to assess whether it is appropriate for this to occur, based on where I am, and then decide if I should let it manifest. This is really no different from holding back a sneeze or any other inappropriate bodily function that might abruptly arise that may need to be contained.

The best description I've come across relative to the phenomena of these sudden bursts of energy came from a book entitled *Kundalini Experience* by Dr. Lee Sanella, in which these sudden jolts were likened to a hose that is bent and thus blocks the flow of water; when suddenly released, the open blockage causes the hose to whip wildly. This is a very accurate depiction of the experience but with bioelectricity rather than water. When these jolts first appeared, I considered them to be a possible neurological disorder, a nervous system tick, or the onset of epilepsy. Not long after they began, I visited a neurologist who suggested that they may be myoclonic jerks, during which my body involuntary twitched or jerked to either release energy or relax before sleep. Eventually, this proved false due to the voluntary control I had over them. I also had an MRI to determine if there was any evidence of a brain tumor or other abnormality. All were negative, and everything, medically, was normal. These electrical shocks were almost immediately assimilated into my conscious awareness, and I made sure they didn't draw undue attention from the people around me. What was further curious about the electrical jolts, jerks, and shocks was that they felt *relieving*. It was as if my body was releasing energy that was building up and needed an open channel, a clear path, a way to reduce growing tension or stress in the inner body. The shocks would eventually trade between local jolts across the body, through the hands, or down the legs to full body jolts when my entire body would unexpectedly explode with powerful live electricity. These electrical manifestations led to a barrage of other experiences that always remained interconnected in new and unusual ways, most notably through sexual energy, which I will outline in the pages to come. This first description introduces the concept of opening up the body to accommodate the energy. Many of the following experiences have that same theme, and that is why I use the word "accommodations." I felt I had to *accommodate* this energy and move out of the way so the energy could flow. This entire process felt like a purification and preparation process. Of course, I had no idea what was to come or why this was happening.

2. Spontaneous Bodily Stretches—Yoga Posturing—Kriyas and Asanas

Not long after the first bioelectrical shocks started firing about my body, another quite strange phenomenon began to occur. Without a preconceived thought or intention, my body would suddenly *need* to rip, stretch, and position itself into postures that I have never experienced before. Although I had done quite a bit of stretching while practicing hatha yoga, Tai Chi, and karate, this was different. As mentioned earlier, it can best be likened to the way our bodies automatically stretch, groan, and reach our arms and hands out when we have a good yawn; the body has an innate kinesthetic knowledge of what it needs to do to accommodate this instinctive bodily need. These postures, also known as kriyas in yoga, have become pervasive throughout my body and have persisted, intensified, and expanded over the course of the years. I clearly remember when I got engaged to Nancy in 1987, we were staying at the Queen Ann Inn Bed and Breakfast in Cape Cod, and I could not stop stretching, twisting, and opening my body up as if it needed to prepare itself for some future state. I felt like the William Hurt character in the movie *Altered States* or Lon Chaney's werewolf transformation in *Wolfman*. Nancy thought I was strange, but I made light of it and simply said I needed to stretch out. I also hid most of the time when this became extreme so she didn't get fed up with the whole thing. I was constantly trying to address all of these experiences in private and not reveal them to anyone—because, privately, I was desperately trying to understand what was happening to me.

These spontaneous automatic postures were impacting my entire body and not localized to one area or body part. In one moment, they would affect my neck, face, mouth, and tongue, and I would suddenly make frightening faces by extensively stretching open my jaw to the point of it hurting. My tongue would also be stretched out as well, making the entire event comical and insane at the same time. The only people I showed these faces to were my kids, Jenna and Richard, because they were young, and I figured I could entertain them while simultaneously accommodating this uncanny need. To this day, they get a kick out of those faces, as they thought they were quite strange, crazy, and funny all at the same time. Their cousins, Christopher and Cassie, were the only other kids I revealed this to. They thought I was nuts—but in a good way (I think).

Although I will describe more about these kriyas later, it's important to note that this was a regular thing—I mean daily. The bioelectrical shocks and the ongoing kriyas became second nature in my private world for decades while they morphed and contorted my body relentlessly. I made a practice of going to the New York Sports Club during this time, where I spent my time stretching and breathing into these yoga-like positions while not actually doing yoga.

3. Collection Breaths and a New Brain and Body Energy State

Soon after the bioelectrical shocks and automatic body movements established themselves as part of this bizarre physical journey, another practice and tendency unfolded, which I came to call "collection breaths." Again, remember that this is my *body* doing all this—*not me.* I was trying to accommodate, adjust, and assimilate these demands of my body as they mysteriously unfolded. It was if alien life was expressing itself from within me, and my mind was desperately trying to figure it out and understand its intelligence and ultimate purpose. I suddenly, and quite instinctively, started taking deep inhalations that would seem to mix with a newly growing sensation in my upper body and brain, creating a distinct experience of being naturally high—literally. This is very difficult to articulate and communicate because it was not with every breath; it occurred only when there was an increased presence of this newly evolving energy in my brain and body that seemed to elicit this specific type of breath. There was a sensation in my body that would trigger this type of inhalation, and it was as though I was collecting a mixing of the air and the energy together to create this new inner blissful state. My brain was experiencing a buzzing high that would transition into a tickling sense of giddiness. I would literally feel drunk, glazed, and tingly. The best correlative experience I can think of was being on nitrous oxide, cannabis, or, in the beginning, a mild laughing gas that later intensified into hysterical laughter, which I will explain in more detail later. As I mentioned, it didn't happen with every breath but only when the body was producing this inner condition from a spontaneous state. The experience became unmistakable to me, and I would try to catch a perfect mixing between the breath and the energy that was beginning to create a quite natural euphoric state or chemistry in my brain and body. This was the beginning of a new inner brain and body chemistry that was simply *not there before* and had *a distinct reality of its own.* It was also the beginning of what would grow into many other future inner states having to do with sexual energy, rapture, and other manifestations I will describe as we move on. For now, there was clearly a connection between the electrical shocks, the automatic body postures, and these collection breaths. These conditions would often converge and create very powerful and transformative inner states. The key, looking back, is that the biochemical physiology of my inner life was literally changing on its own accord. Historically, yogis and other practices of energy development referred to the energy that involved breath as *prana.* It might also be noted that breathing patterns have always played a large role in meditation and stress reduction. It is one of the many ways all this connects together. I want to add at this juncture that these were not all wonderful joyful experiences. They were at times very uncomfortable and distressing. In their most extreme manifestations they were frightening and concerning.

4. Snapping, Crackling, Crunching, and Popping

Another quite strange bodily phenomenon started close to the same time as the first three. Consider the common and familiar experience of cracking your knuckles. If you pay close attention, it sounds and feels as if nerves, joints, and bones are snapping and crackling. Although this phenomenon appears to be a quite simple bodily experience that science understands, it actually isn't well understood. Different theories suggest that bubbles of certain bodily fluids pop, or a cavity of space is suddenly filled, or ligaments crunch or snap when extended. In my case, for reasons I still cannot comprehend, this phenomenon pervaded my face, jaw, neck, and hands. For some reason, my body needs to crackle, pop, and snap through these body parts. Once again, my body involuntarily did this, but I almost immediately managed to have voluntary control over it. This again meant that I could feel a premonition and have a split second to decide if it was appropriate to manifest. I would not include this bizarre activity in these writings if it was just an idiosyncrasy that many people have. I felt as though I were relieving some inner condition that I didn't understand. But again, it felt good, right, and necessary as part of this newly evolving physical state. Again, when alone, I would look at my hands while I intentionally made this phenomenon happen. These odd experiences soon became tied to the automatic postures I mentioned earlier and were consistent with the idea that my body was going through a metamorphosis of a specific kind and *somehow knew what it was doing.* Since this is the first time I'm attempting to put this in writing for others to read, I'm finding the experience slightly uncomfortable, humorous, and just plain crazy too, yet it is all true and quite real. As one might expect, my wife, Nancy, was horrified with this new tendency of mine, while my two children, Jenna and Richard, found it curious, weird, and funny. It became just another little quirk that their slightly strange dad displayed.

5. The Opening of Circuits and Accommodating a Distinct Flow of Energy

In Tai Chi, I was taught to keep the body in posture while maintaining a soft, even flow of movement. For example, the back needed to be kept in alignment, the neck had to be held straight, and the hands needed to be open and relaxed with the thumb slightly pointing out. Tai Chi is all about the flow of energy in the body but requires that one's attention stay focused on the tendency to shift out of the posture, tense up, and drift off into a mechanical mental narrative. While the practice of this physical art helped build my body and prepare it to withstand a more powerful level of energy, it also helped me to foster a mental habit of paying attention by uncritically correcting posture in order to maximize this flow. My attention is almost always scanning the body for tension, correcting posture, breathing consciously, and positioning it for optimal openness. Eventually I came to use this same practice of automatic correction relative to my emotions, ego, and distracted mind as we will see later.

Soon after many of these extreme bodily changes started manifesting, I began to experience another phenomenon relative to the sensation of energy itself and its movement in the body. One of the first places I recall this happening was in the hands. I would suddenly feel a vague buildup of discomfort/pressure in my hands that I could only accommodate and relieve by opening the hands, stretching out the fingers, relaxing them fully, and then bending the hands back to almost a ninety-degree angle. This specific positioning and posturing of both hands would create a distinct sensation, as if a circuit was now opening in the wrists and allowing energy to flow. This practice would relieve the buildup and create a distinct sensation of filling the hands with a mysterious energy. What was clear was that this was not just a warm tingle that most of us feel when we relax our hands, but instead, it felt like a specific energy flow was filling my hands and electrifying them. It was that same experience that I explained in the earlier manifestations, in which my inner body was filling with a powerful, electrical, and transformative current. The concept of "opening a circuit" fit precisely and was repeated in other parts of the body, including the face, neck, ankles, and feet. Most specifically, as this phenomenon advanced and progressed, I would bend my head back, rip open the muscles in my neck, shift my head back and forth, and feel a euphoric high enter my brain (much like the kriyas mentioned earlier). There was also a distinct experience that has been documented in Tai Chi and yoga in which I would place the tip of my tongue behind the front teeth on the roof of my mouth and feel an electrical stream pass through that particular spot. This would eventually contribute to other sensations and effects that I will describe later, but clearly, something major was going on that had an agenda and intelligence all of its own. The important point is that these new sensations were being created by a kind of energetically charged, transformative chemistry. The idea of there being potentially a reality to spiritual alchemy becomes quite believable. Our bodies are an inconceivable mix of chemistry, energy, and physiology, and there very well might be new potentials that lie dormant in all of us. The fact that nature can produce the venom of a snake or the toxic odor from a skunk should wake us up to the potential of all possibilities and, again, not surprise us.

6. Mysterious Electrochemical Energy

This sensation of a certain type of energetically charged, transformative chemistry became more pronounced as time (years) went on. The experience of a flow of energy surreptitiously started to feel more like actual electrically charged energy that was alive and moving in my body. This specific experience would become a most profound and extraordinary development in that I could feel it literally in the tissues of my body as it simultaneously appeared to be rewiring a certain dimension of the electrical network that ran my nervous system. It was as if the original electrical shocks that spontaneously triggered in my early twenties were the early stirrings of what would become a lifelong unfolding of whatever the totality of this experience was to become. All the other experiences—automatic movements, collection breaths, nerve popping, and the opening of circuits— were a precursor of what was to come. What I eventually realized was that even the commencement of my intellectual search was part of this same process, although quite hidden from me at the time. The critical key at this point is that the experience was chemical, electrical, and visceral and that it was clear that this energy communicated with itself in a highly coordinated and almost preprogrammed manner. As you might sense, I was playing a part of a scientist trying to understand a phenomenon that was occurring in me. I read every book I could find on the subject but did not find anything exactly like it. There were no external answers I could find that satisfied me, and it continues to this day. I still make no claims of understanding all this, so if you are skeptical, intrigued, or cynical, we share all these experiences together. One must keep an ever-open mind with life.

7. Activation Levels and Phasing—An Extreme Intensity

The activation levels of these experiences vary on their own volition. By activation level, I mean that the currents of energy could either become extremely active and disturbing, have a medium or subtle presence in the body, or become calm yet blissfull. I came to call this "phasing." Phasing refers to the fact that this living, moving, and evolving force of energy vacillates according to rhythm and pattern of its own programming and exhibits an extraordinary order of intelligence that is pursuing some pre-ordained course, without being clear and distinct. I divided the varying levels of intensity and activation into three phases. The first phase I identified as having no perceptible physical activity except for a pervasive soft energetic presence, or, in other words, being almost totally normal. The second phase was when the Kundalini was active and clearly present as either flowing or highly euphoric to the point where I could not help noticing it in my body and brain. The third phase was when the condition became highly activated and almost menacingly disruptive in a barrage of ways. In this third phase of high activity, I encountered some distinctly harrowing experiences and states that would last sometimes for hours. This highly active state would often elevate the shocks, the ripping open of circuits, the collection breaths, the crackling and popping of joints. In addition, there might also be extreme sexual energy, spontaneous eruptive laughter, or a need to walk, move, or drive. There had to be motion, or it was too much for me to withstand. There would also be fits of creativity during which I would improvise on my guitar, write in a journal, or, most often, listen to music. I understand that much of this sounds fun and great, which it was and is, but I had no outlet to express any of this with anyone and was frightened that something out of control was happening to me. I found myself questioning my identity and experiencing an uprising of anxiety and, at passing moments, a pending panic that, while intimidating, never went over the limit that could have caused insanity. During these very heightened and intense times, I would direct my attention toward positive ideas, ponder observations and connections, and use many relaxation and centering methods I had learned over the years. It was also during these times when I would ingest esoteric teachings I had studied my entire life in the form of books, talks, videos, and live meetings and discussions. I was fortunate that I experienced the lower mind states that were frantic and childish. I was used to the presence of an unintelligent maniac in my mind and head that was largely idiotic and baseless. At times, it might get the better of me but was ultimately no match for the wisdom of higher consciousness. All this helped to placate the intensity of this phase. Overall, I did remain centered and at peace, as I always had that almost paranormal relationship with life (the company I referred to earlier) and the mysterious unknown that was comforting and reassuring. In these revved and amped inner states, I always felt overwhelming gratitude and spiritual connectedness with what most would call God, for which I felt a wordless sense of reverent silence. This extreme phase became so familiar and expected that they eventually like any other condition that recurs in our ever-changing bodies. "Here we go again," would often play in my head. In this later phase in my life, the extreme state has become even more prominent and constant; I would say that as of July of 2019 this state occupies a minimum of 4-8 hours a day.

8. Extreme Sleepiness Episodes and Freezing Water

During the highly active phases, this distinct experience of electrical energy that was roaring into my brain and nervous system caused many other odd manifestations. One that challenged me repeatedly was a highly specific form of sleepiness. It was not the ordinary sleepiness we all feel, or I would not mention it, and it's also not correlated to the fact that I woke up at 3:00 a.m. religiously without an alarm. I would fall asleep quickly (much to my wife's chagrin), sleep solidly (much to wife's chagrin), and wake up without the slightest effort (much to my wife's chagrin). At times during the day, with no predictability at all, these bouts of sleepiness would become overwhelming and would be very difficult to shake. It would be as though a spell had been cast on my brain, and my eyes would glaze over, and eyelids would literally flutter and almost be forced shut. This condition would also activate very deep and elongated yawns that were extended and abnormal. There is something about the act of yawning, based on my experience, that I believe is not yet known. I would have bizarre yawning fits that would radically alter my breathing and engage my entire body. Again, this felt as though there was an abnormal presence in a section of my brain that brought on sleep, yawning, and breath alteration. There is much more about this state, but it is almost too difficult to put into words and might sound repetitive. The bottom line is that these states would not go away with a simple nap and often became even more intense *after a nap*. This manifestation remains a mystery, as I would spend, sometimes hours, battling this state by swimming, taking ice showers, walking briskly, and stretching. Putting my head and face in freezing water seemed to help what felt like a boiling hot brain when I was in this hyperactive state. Ultimately, I came to observe that this condition was not restricted to regions of my brain, although, due to the heavy sleepiness that I would feel, it seemed like it was solely in the brain. This condition was actually pervading my entire body, but its effect in the brain was to induce ongoing sleepiness. The rest of my body, during these intense phases, would jolt, crackle, pop, stretch, yawn, and enact the kriyas and extreme postures mentioned above. It was all interconnected in an extraordinary way, but there was no logic that I could apply that made sense. Over the years, I thought maybe I suffered from narcolepsy and a mild form of epilepsy, but these conditions take full involuntary control of the body. I was managing them consciously. There was also the stark reality that all these other oddball experiences I have listed were not mentioned under the medical descriptions of those conditions. One last point I would add to this manifestation is that I have recently been studying literature from writers and researhers like Dr. Joe Dispenza and Dr. Rick Strassmen who are exploring the Pineal Gland which is both connected to higher experience and levels of melatonin which impacts the circadian rhythms that are directly related to wakefulness and sleepiness. There is an entire science evolving around the biological basis of spiritual experience and they are at the very forefront. I cannot go into those details at this time but it is a subject of future exploration and an area I intend on delving deeper into in the very near future.

9. Brain Nausea, Drug-like States, and Alterations in Physiology

It is concerning when one's very physiology is being altered in real time (right before our very eyes). I had simply never experienced these things, and they just kept coming. I can liken it to a drug experience because, while it had many positive effects, it also had complicated and disturbing effects. One such impact on the brain was that I would develop a certain type of nausea that seemed centralized in the brain yet didn't influence hunger or the desire for food. My stomach played no part in it, and I never got sick. It felt as if the electrical currents in my brain were disrupting the neurons and tissue just enough to make me feel this strange type of nausea. These states didn't last long, were less frequent than the others, and disappeared over time. The fact that this felt as though I had taken an actual drug is intriguing. If we think about it, when we ingest any drug, it alters the very physiology of the cells of our bodies. If indeed a new biochemical agent in the form of energy was affecting my body, then I am simply reporting on its effects. As to its potential danger, I had no choice but *to trust that life knew what it was doing* based on its extraordinary track record. The key was whether or not this total condition was a malady or a transformation. For my own sanity, I remember recalling nature's capability of creating new physiology that was beneficial and useful, and I hoped that perhaps this was a living example of just such a change. My everyday attention had become used to handling these bizarre changes in my biophysiology. My inner world was like an ongoing Marx Brothers movie that I watched, laughed with, noted in my journals, and continuously collected notes on to add to my understanding and comprehension of the totality.

10. Uncontainable Laughter, Sexual Energy, and Ecstatic Joy

As if the experiences I have described already did not create enough strangeness and disruption, the experience involving laughter started to occur after more than twenty years into these experiences. What started to manifest as giddiness during the strange onsets of euphoria would sometimes turn into uproarious and uncontrollable laughter—and I am talking about a belly laugh in which the body is completely intoxicated with hysteria. This was not occurring because of a joke or a funny story; this was like LSD or mescaline suddenly flooding into the brain and bloodstream. It felt as if a chemical laughter bomb went off in my body that was impossible to suppress (not that I wanted to). This is a curious phenomenon but something we can all relate to if we recall the drunk-like experience in our bodies and brains when we laugh hysterically, feel giddy, or experience a good high. Even without a highly charged Kundalini experience, most people have had these experiences and should pay attention to the change in their body chemistry when in this state, because it contains many useful revelations. My perspective is that human physiology is already equipped with profound potential and is aching to expand these energies with the right life conduct. There is an extraordinary future in this. Meticulous management of our inner chemistry and energy mixed with the right use of evolved self-observation could lead to an extraordinary dimension of human experience.

This jovial, buzzing, tingling laughter condition started to mix with sexual energy, which was already quite powerful. There is no doubt that creative energy and sexual energy are inseparably linked, but they can both synthesize into an entirely new bio-energetic experience that, when combined, timed, and aligned with an orgasm, can blast open new pathways for higher energies to flow openly through our system. A distinct change that occurred incrementally over time was the voltage of energy and impact on my body's sexual energy. Because I already had a deep respect for the science behind life's creative process, I was able to let go and release these intense eruptions without being concerned that they might cause harm. Like laughter, most people experience sexual energy, and if we think of the pervasive pleasure and the shocking electrical charge of an orgasm, it is hard not to think that we are all wired for a lot more potential in this area. At its most extreme manifestation, these sexual experiences caused the most powerful jolts, aftershocks, and out-of-control laughter I ever experienced.

The practice of Tantric yoga and other esoteric practices that focus on sexual energy have been around for a long time. The idea of cultivating sexual energy into a higher constitution of itself is not at all new. Hundreds of books have been written about this topic; it's just not mainstream. Our aim should be to move in the direction of optimally conducting our lives to provide the most ideal inner conditions for our fullest and healthiest sexual potential to be realized. As time pressed on over the decades, these experiences changed and expanded, and the rush that accompanied the ecstatic states always offered new surprises (at times the laughter became so extreme it was almost frightening). Sex, laughter, fun, joy, and exploring new ground is a lethal combination – I can only advise that orgasms have a super potential that can transform in our life-time. This energy should be used as validation of higher states and I can attest that my physiology has changed and is not what it was decades ago (this is profound and ominous).

11. Whipping Body Movements, Dancing, Shaking, and Jumping Moves the Energy Dynamically

Clearly, the central theme of these entries is that higher energy had become activated, and the body needed to comply with its new demands. If for a moment we step back and look objectively at yoga postures or the practices of Tai Chi and Chi Kung, we see that humanity has created entire movement systems that optimize and accommodate an active flow of energy. Advanced meditation and coordinated breathing accomplish a similar end. While I covered this idea in the section on kriyas and automatic postures and contortions, there is also the phenomenon of whipping motions, dancing, shaking, and jumping. Before I address this in more detail, consider the strange tribal dances and wild shaking you might have seen in indigenous people in remote parts of the world. Consider the distinct possibility that their bodies excitedly dance because they are very much in touch with the raw natural power of nature and are free to let go, and it allows it to flow without cultural taboos. Great dancers of all types become very uninhibited when dancing, although they may quickly fall back under the spell of society once they are off the dance floor (or off the table).

In my case, I started to channel the jolts and movement of energy through relaxed limbs, which I learned from practicing Tai Chi. Techniques in Chi Kung also helped facilitate these movements, and soon I found myself whipping my arms back, jumping up and down, or moving the body quickly in dancelike motions. I practiced these techniques mostly in my room at home; I had a large blanket and mat on the floor where I did most of my energy exercises. I had full control of these movements, which seemed to serve the purpose of moving the energy through more channels in the body. My best guess is that this energy was preparing the body for more advanced levels of the quality and quantity of the Kundalini as it opened more circuits. Classical Kundalini models speak in terms of energy moving up the chakras, which I would imagine is similar to these experiences; however, I never experienced a distinct linear rising. To me, it felt like the energy was wildly exploring every open route it could find no matter where it was—including my brain. It was more of a dynamic frenzy than an orderly, logical, step-by-step process—although it was supremely intelligent. After these intense energy practices, I would feel as if the energy was reverberating in a freer, happier, and more liberated state. When I effectively galvanized the energy, it often remained with me well into the day, and I found myself making efforts to not telegraph any strangeness to others. I became a wizard at hiding these quirky manifestations, as I had to maintain a façade of being a salesman. My inner life would often become quite wild with inner currents, uproarious emotion, and sudden bioelectrical jolts. It is important to remember that a major theme of my life and this book was living this dual life and managing these experiences throughout the day. It is important that we all explore our own inner psychological secret private world and how we become such masters at not letting other people know our deeper selves. When we are managing strange physical experiences (good or bad), or managing our inner voices while making sure we don't accidentally expose ourselves, it takes consciousness and awareness. A healthy practice for us all is to let that inner self out and let it flow in private (and sometimes in public) and make our life more of an ongoing inner jamboree of fun. (Hey, as I see it, being crazy, creative, and kooky is far less boring than most of external life.) As a quick note regarding this entry, it might be entertaining to note that I am not at all a good dancer in the classic sense (much to my wife's chagrin). I am actually awful. My wife and both kids are great dancers who appear to be the ones who are free-spirited and charged with electricity. I have been told I dance like Frankenstein and have no natural rhythm. Just thought I would mention this small fact in case I was giving the impression that I am an acrobatic and extraordinary dancer. I am not, however, in private, when accommodating Kundalini, I can look like a Voodoo tribesman on enhanced LSD.

12. Inconceivable Bliss Waves

Probably the most elusive of all these manifestations was an indescribable inner emission of bliss that spontaneously filled my body. Although this happened several times over the years, it varied in intensity. During a long walk one morning, I experienced a sudden release of blissful electrical energy while under a tree at a park near my house. This was not an ordinary wave of joy, and it was different from the blissful states I had experienced previously. This wave was silent and overpowering and became branded in my memory in an unusual way. I never forgot it. It emerged from deep within, filled my body for several seconds, and then magically subsided, leaving me in peaceful awe. I remember clearly that there was absolutely nothing that could be said in words, and I felt a state of pure consciousness and bliss *and nothing else.* I remember describing the state (to myself) as like a full body orgasm through a completely relaxed body. If I try any harder to explain this, I might do it a disservice, so I need to leave it at that.

In addition to these waves, which I did not have control over, my body would also sometimes generate involuntarily inner experiences so off the charts and beyond ordinary expression that there was simply no choice but to intellectually note it and move on. For me, some of these moments were downright frightening. I remember on more than one occasion the feeling of having the beginning of a heart attack or that my body was suddenly shutting down to die. When we don't know what is happening, our minds concoct paranoid fears that are downright terrifying. Experiences like these teach us that our bodily chemistry and energy is so beyond human understanding and science today that we should be open to the incomprehensible nature of life and the potential that exists in our own bodies. We should not underestimate what might be possible and should be humble to its potential. The fact that our bodies produce such an extraordinary state should pique our interest and should not be overlooked. We spend so much time spiritually weakened by anxiety, depression, hopelessness, and worry that we barely remember our highest states. When we consider the inner states resulting from laughter, sex, love, connectedness to nature, the joy of animals, learning new things, and exploring new places, it is all so positive, yet we are often pulled deeper into misery than unfathomable joy. So many people suffer mentally when there is absolutely no physical threat or reason to. We almost purposely reach for bad memories or future worries without examining how ludicrous it is. We think it is normal or that we must suffer over this and pay a penance—but why? To whom? Our own imagination? This is part of what awakening is—awakening to the fact that our normal mind is largely an unexamined lunatic that suffers from our self-contrived fears, hostilities, and self-pity. Consider leisurely walking and whistling about, enmired in our mental voices of suffering, and suddenly a Doberman Pinscher tears out at us from behind a fence! Observe for yourself, even in this imaginary story, how those voices in your head instantly vanish. They no longer exist, and a split second ago, those voices were tormenting us about some future possibility that will never happen. How much of our lives are spent in this hypnotic stream of fabrications? What would our lives be like if our consciousness was clear, permeating, and discriminated between absurd thoughts and what is actually happening?

13. Alterations in Health and Well-Being

This entry can be viewed as not a direct manifestation of Kundalini, in the sense that millions of people today are working toward a higher level of health and well-being. A growing number of people are conscious of weight loss; more people belong to a gym; and far more people are meditating, practicing yoga, or attending spas and retreats. Although this trend is not global as of yet, there are certain parts of the world where this lifestyle has been incorporated into the culture. I refer to this as the collective evolution of humanity in contrast to the individual evolution, but they are clearly linked; as individuals evolve, the collective evolves. This is clear evidence that humanity is evolving, contrary to what our automatic minds might think.

The trend toward better health is a sign of a certain level of conscious evolution because we are seeking a better internal state, which in turn will help transform our emotional and mental states. This is a growing trend, as more people seek counseling, read books, and watch videos on eating better, living better, and staying healthy. What is most important relative to Kundalini activation and conscious evolution is that they intuitively require a healthy base from which to grow. It is common that people who seek a higher level of consciousness instinctively know to stop smoking, cut down on toxins, and attend to their health and well-being. As discussed in the first section of the book, I was fortunate to be part of a holistic health center that positioned its entire philosophy on this idea by providing services (acupuncture, chiropractic, herbs, massage therapy) and classes on physical practices like yoga and martial arts. The psychological system I studied relative to conscious evolution referred to a concept called "balanced man," which basically outlined the fact that a human being, in order to increase consciousness, would need to work on the three key centers of body, emotions, and mind in order to optimally work on consciousness and spirituality. To be clear, one need not be the picture of health, since we are all born with many irreversible conditions. It is more about accepting ourselves reasonably and doing whatever we can to be as healthy as possible given the cards we are dealt. People who have more of a spiritual aim usually do not take health *too* seriously because they are cognizant of how it all ends. To spend our life guilty, aggravated, and constantly deprived leaves us basically miserable, with no energy to direct toward other aspirations. Obsessing over health is tiresome and ultimately a losing proposition; we must keep it in perspective. To be tormented by our own health defeats the whole purpose of trying to be healthy. The ideal of course is to live a very healthy life, whatever you feel is your highest attainment of good health, and pursue higher experience from there.

Relative specifically to Kundalini activation, the body knows that it needs to gravitate toward better health—*and often does*. Historically, yogis become vegetarians, meditate regularly, and tend to have a strong respect for nature and animal life. While I personally have lived a relatively healthy life, I haven't gone to an extreme and do not advocate any specific diet or exercise. There is no silver bullet, and everyone is different and should work that out for themselves. What is important from the viewpoint of individual evolution is that we work as much on our emotional and mental development as our body. This is more difficult because many people are not clear on how to work on these centers, and it is not the purpose of this book to go into details on such matters. Clearly, the approach should include moving away from extreme negative emotion and extreme negative thinking, as discussed at the end of the last entry.

The bottom line is that a healthy life tends to nourish the reverence for life, and the reverence of life leads to higher life. Kundalini thrives on increased freedom from all impediments in all of its forms in order to operate at peak efficiency. What is important to this discussion is that the brilliance of life has an innate appreciation and knowledge about how it must prepare the body for this higher energy, whether through acute Kundalini activation or a higher individual life of peace of mind and inner contentment. As will be discussed later in the book, there are extraordinary futuristic developments taking shape now that will completely transform human potential as our ingenious technology merges and partners with higher consciousness to offer a bright and hopeful future.

14. Walks

It is difficult to describe the impossible *need* I developed to take walks. While this entry may be debatable on whether it is connected directly to Kundalini, it became clear to me that walking *and pondering specific issues in a disciplined manner* became essential for my sanity. The physical energy in the body was constantly rising and intensifying and virtually demanding that I get up, get out, and simply – *walk*. These walks could be as short as 20 minutes but often, and religiously every weekend, they would be 90 minutes. The mind would always have 5-10 highlighted issues to observe, connect, and elaborate on. I mentioned these practices earlier in how I interlaced this need to think through ideas while working in the city and how the walks and pondering were inseparable. The ultimate effect was that the combination of being out in nature, breathing fresh air, and keeping the body in motion, all fueled and helped balance the energies in the body which delivered great relief. It distinctly felt as if the simultaneous movement of the body, the open flow of emotion, and the intellectual engagement in self development became a soothing holistic practice. The key elevation that the walks provided was an open mind to scale multiple possibilities at once and consider how everything interconnects. Every walk resulted in a deeper understanding of the whole.

15. Extraordinary Pervasiveness

This final entry is perhaps the most profound because it is the most recent and therefore is both collective and encompassing. It is the consummation of the totality of this experience and is most astonishing. The simple fact is that there is a cohesive intelligence that is pervasive to the entirety of the bio-cellular changes in the physiology. My brain, nervous system, emotions, and mind are all being bio-neuro-chemically altered. This is not hearsay, a flight of mental fantasy, or wishful thinking – this is as scientifically measurable as the changes in a woman's body when pregnant. The heavy presence of the energy in my head that causes these severe bouts of sleepiness and heat appears to be exactly the same energy causing the jolts, the kriyas, the hysterical laughter, the alterations in breathing, and all the other physical and literal changes. I can observe directly these unusual bio-cellular alterations and pan across my body and experiences as one single unified order of intelligence and creation. It is not haphazard, accidental, or chaotic. There is brilliant design in what appears to me as impossible. The fact that it is pervasive and not localized is riveting. The strangest part of it is that there continues to be a mental battle over its ultimate nature and mysterious presence in what appears to be a limited number of people (which I could be and hope, I am wrong about). To this day I cross-examine the experience in an attempt to gain a fuller and deeper understanding of this challenging reality.

Kundalini's Sweeping Impact on Emotion

Higher Energies Transform Our Emotional Constitution through Spirituality, Art, Music, Movies, Theater, Humor, and Relationships

As we delve deeper into the *experience* of this transformation through Kundalini energy, I want to explore how emotions came to play a major role in fueling and feeding my drive and desire to continue on this path. In order to do so, I want to circle back to the start of my psychological search as a teenager. If we recall, my question of existence refined itself into the following: *what is the ultimate potential of human experience?* I was confounded by where life ultimately leads and curious about what higher realms of experience a human being is designed to explore and realize in his or her lifetime. My drive to understand our existence consumed my mind and consciousness. I came to pleasantly realize over time that there was one all-encompassing spirit that was enlivening the entire search and exploration from the start, and it was that *I simply loved life* and wanted to understand its mystery, nature, and purpose to my utmost potential. That was the driving force behind everything I had experienced and why I defined a spiritual relationship to life as being filled with awe and reverence *to existence and life itself.* What propelled my search, though, was the fact that so much in everyday life contradicts this perspective. It is the classic and familiar *good versus evil* that relentlessly challenges all of us. Life can appear just as evil as it appears wonderful, and as wonderful as it appears evil. The two extremes are equally polarized, which makes life gut-wrenching for all of us (unless one alters consciousness itself). I have come to understand that making sense of the apparent injustices and emotionally painful experiences in life is virtually impossible from our ordinary level of thinking. On the one hand, we find life to be brilliant, intelligent, and beautiful, and on the other, it seems hopelessly unfair and absolutely mad. We can go crazy trying to reconcile Hitler and Bin Laden to a Buddha and Jesus. Many people either never dare approach this paradox or simply follow a religion or belief system without questioning and probing *for themselves.* Other people, like me, and possibly you, need to delve deeper into the mystery. I reject the dogmatic, mechanical, and repetitious worship of God in favor of a search for higher understanding. In my case, this search for something more ignited because I was mystified by the entire gambit of life, and this mystery manifested for me in many ways across a variety of experiences. It has been the endless enjoyment of the actual search itself that has been the fulfillment and not in obtaining *"an answer"* from the universe. In other words, it is not as if I found one final answer that answered my question and resolved my curiosity. Far from it. It is more about nourishing a living and open-ended relationship with life that is interactive and ever surprising and profound. To experience life with an attitude of conclusiveness became blasphemous to me. A conclusion is a sign of death or, at the very least, ignorance. When one lives from "conclusions" one is doomed to defend and uphold them which invite perpetual mental strife and frustration.

As the Kundalini energy in me sought to actualize itself in any way it could, it had a definitive impact on my emotions. Emotional energy can be derived and developed through many mediums, and the nature of Kundalini energy is to be eclectic and open to all possibilities. In the following pages, I will recount and detail the specific ways that Kundalini further nourished itself emotionally through spirituality, art, music, movies, theater, humor, and relationships with people. Again, we all derive a much-needed energy lift from such mediums, but I believe there is more going on than meets the eye, and I want to make this point by inviting you into the specific details of my experience. I am outlining this detail only as an example; *your* personal joys, hobbies, and entertainment furnish *you* with *your* energy. *Your* journey is unique to *you*. I can only recommend aggressive introspection, identifying the emotional catalysts for your own evolution, and managing your life in a way that maximizes these streams of passion. As you read through the following pages, enjoy the process of asking yourself why you are drawn to certain forms of entertainment and what you think *you* get out of them, other than the obvious. The obvious is boring. The key idea to keep in mind through these seven segments is that there is a single thread that runs through all of them. That single thread *is how we lift our own energy up in an optimistic and positive manner through the brilliant creativity that life itself is furnishing for this very purpose.* Keep in mind that human creativity is an extension of the creativity of nature and life itself; in other words, spirituality, music, art, movies, theater, humor, and relationships are new channels for life to grow and evolve *through and with us.* We need to use them, enjoy them, and parlay them into our personal self-elevation. Therefore, do not get sidetracked if you don't share my tastes. That is not the point. Try to explore your own proclivities with an adventurous spirit. You also may not recognize or know my references. Again, that is fine because it is the idea that is driving my point.

Spirituality

Spirituality is beautiful. To be spiritual suggests a deeper and more meaningful existence that is steeped in love, joy, and gratitude. Spirituality is also directly associated with a relationship to the sacred and supernatural. This dimension of life is often missed by many people for a variety of reasons, but if we are fortunate enough to feel such an allure, then we owe it to ourselves to explore it to its fullest potential. Without an emotional connection to simply *being alive*, we are restricted in the range of higher experience that is available to us.

In my case, I was fortunate to connect to nature, which led to a deeply felt kinship and inner comfort with life. Being surrounded by the massive and ominous living intelligence of life easily overpowered my ordinary mind, but being alone in nature served as a reassuring anchor no matter what happened in the outside world (even if sometimes it took a little time to come back to nature and peace). Before we consider Kundalini in how it further lifted this experience for me, I want to add another part of my past that contributed to this spiritual dimension of my life. At Fordham University, we were required to take classes in theology and religion, and thus I was introduced to mysticism. Because I was already interested in the potential of human experience and specifically the highest possible inner states of humanity, I was instantly fascinated by certain mystics and saints. Specifically, I was drawn to St. Francis of Assisi, who had an affinity for nature and animals and saw all living things as divine reflections of God. This relationship empowered his mission, kept him in an enraptured state, and inspired him throughout his life. As my Kundalini energy experiences grew and my consciousness expanded, I was filled with overflowing gratitude, which moved me to write this book and share my experiences. At the time of taking the classes at Fordham, I had no medium to communicate what I was experiencing and thus let it build over decades. This book is actually my first attempt to reach out and communicate my experiences and transformation, with the idea of helping anyone who might be drawn to its content. It took me a long while before I found my voice, but everyone's fate is different. A spiritual relationship with life is a living interaction that lives and breathes as long as we actively feed and nourish it—without it we succumb to misery and despair which are philosophic dead-ends. To consider one-self "spiritual" does not imply being "religious" but it does not preclude it either. One can evolve one's spirituality with religious experiences that range over every conceivable facet of one's life. Being spiritually oriented toward life is to live in reverence, respect, and silent adoration for the cosmos, plants, animals, and the ultimate evolution of the integrity of humanity—it is the experiencing *everything* from the point of view of—US.

Art

As I alluded to in the second section of the book, a lot of the spectacular creativity has been channeled through life's evolution into the consciousness and *hands* of humanity. If we stop and envision the enormous breadth of creativity found in the universe and nature that pours through the artistry of humanity, we will be astounded by the masterpieces in art and music from this perspective. In the case of art, and I do not profess to be a connoisseur of art on any level, I have been personally drawn to Michelangelo and Leonardo da Vinci because of the degree of genius that manifests through their work. The sense of awe that their accomplishments inspired in me are identical to the way nature's creations drew my intrigue. To me, the silk and design of the spiderweb were no different from the paint and paintings of these artists—an absolutely different scale of course, but even *the paint* is a creative accomplishment through humanity, as are the results of the use of the paint. For me, all of this served to ignite that same evolutionary impulse to grow using this powerful energy of Kundalini. I could feel the energy reverberating in me, as most people do, when I appreciated the marvel of this level of creativity. This is why art is so universally compelling to people. It is the sense of *connectedness we feel inside ourselves* when we see such masterpieces, not the masterpiece itself. In other words, it is the relationship of our living consciousness with the creativity that channeled through the artist at the time of its manifestation.

Another favorite artist of mine is Alex Grey. I mentioned earlier that, as a salesman in New York City, I had many spots and places I frequented that fed my aim and interest in consciousness and energy. One such place was the East West Bookstore on Fifth Avenue. Although this bookstore no longer exists, it specialized in spirituality, meditation, and esoteric writings from every culture. One day in the 1990s, I was browsing the bookstore when a book cover leaped out at me and exploded in my brain. It was called *Sacred Mirrors: The Visionary Art of Alex Grey*. On the cover of this rather large book was a stark depiction of divine and spiritual energy emanating out of a human brain and head, with striking and beautiful colors and precise detail of human physiology. Alex Grey's art is a stunningly accurate depiction of my experience of Kundalini energy and how it is flawlessly correlated to the complex anatomy of the body—something I wondered about all the time. I became instantly enamored of his work and adorned my office at home with his books, paintings, and postcards. I even ultimately wrote parts of this book in a place he opened with his wife, Allyson (also a brilliant artist), in Upstate New York called COSM (Chapel of Sacred Mirrors), which not only features their work and special events but offers rooms to stay overnight. Alex has mastered the visionary art of depicting how consciousness and energy are interconnected through one supreme intelligence and as one mystical force of infinite creation. Again, the value of art, in this case, is to show how the internal Kundalini/creative inner energies intuitively and magnetically find such perfect mediums to embolden, reaffirm, and invigorate themselves. It becomes increasingly more powerful by manifesting through such artists. Alex Grey's art inspired me, but the world of art offers virtually endless potential for the tastes of each and every person. If you do not see yourself as an art lover, think again; once I realized how good I felt inside every time I picked up a favorite album cover and design I loved, I realized I always loved art. Look around and attend to how *you feel* when you see things *you* love. It could be a book cover, a poster, a building, your home, a picture of a loved one, and on and on. It's all art and flaming one's own appreciation of art and creativity elevates one's energy and therefore our own creativity.

Music

Music has a very special place in my exploration of conscious evolution and Kundalini optimization. My infatuation with guitar playing in my teens helped me to appreciate astounding musicians who displayed uncanny talent. While I was drawn mostly to the creativity and style of Jimmy Page of Led Zeppelin, it was Jimi Hendrix who sent me off in a different orbit regarding music. His guitar playing and how the creative flow of intelligence moved through him seemed totally unworldly. It was clear when I listened to his music and watched him play that it was as if life's radiant brilliance was directly channeling through him (much like Michelangelo and da Vinci), and he was openly receiving and delivering this creative force that far transcended him and everyone listening to him. *It was numbing and chilling to behold.* I couldn't help wondering about the nature of life and existence as a result of this extraordinariness, and it was a segue into being philosophical about music that made the difference. To enjoy music and discuss music is one thing, but to allow intelligence to look at music as almost a spooky manifestation of creativity is quite another. *Have you ever considered music to be spooky?* I am not talking about spooky music; I am talking about the very presence of music on this planet. To me, it was like pure magic manifesting before my eyes. This captivation and connection later spread to many other forms of music, as the experience of listening *to the right music* for *the right inner state* became an art I mastered over time. I made a point of making playlists on my iPod that had similar vibrational effects on my nervous system and used them to alter my moods and supercharge positive states of being. While the music ranged from rock, to blues, to reggae, to jazz, to, most recently, rap and pop, the other most profound experience came from Beethoven's Ninth Symphony. Again, because I had a cerebral bent and enjoyed the sheer ecstasy of music, I found this particular piece of music to be virtually impossible to have come from the same humanity that can be so hateful, violent, and overtly unconscious. The music lifted me out of mundane and predictable states of mind, and I used it to nourish the positive energy that Kundalini was delivering. *The important theme is that when higher energies become activated in us, our consciousness is raised to a more evolved state that becomes temporarily expanded, which is life itself growing through the activation of new neural connections.* Without knowing it, we are all enriching our energy when we avail ourselves to music, art, dance, and just about any creative manifestation that makes us feel good. What we see is that there is a hierarchy of the levels of creativity that life manifests, and it is always exploring new incarnations of this cosmic creativity through our lives. To connect the intelligence of creativity to the very music we listen to daily is transformational. Music is like having a drug enter your system, through your ears, that alters your very cells and elevates your state of being. We ought to connect our lives to that source in a more intentional and deliberate manner. The point I am making is that all creativity, in all its arrays of incarnations, is life's way of sharing the celebration of being alive. When we can hear and feel that energy in every form of music from Eminem, to Frank Sinatra, to Radiohead and Tool, to the soundtrack to *Mary Poppins*, we are beginning to understand life's true interconnected glory. On my iPod, I would often set the device on random and would revel in listening to "Supercalifragilisticexpialidocious" from the Mary Poppins soundtrack, to "Gin and Juice" by Snoop Dogg, to a Bach fugue—*and smile*. It is life *in the music* that becomes our infatuation, not any one particular song or artist. It is living creativity unleashing without bounds that become limited only by our own narrow tastes. In the exploding array of new music that is flooding into the world today we are seeing a trend I find fascinating and worthy of attention. Although artists have collaborated in the past; today, established musical geniuses are making more music together to form an entirely new dimension. While this is happening largely in pop and rap (Jay Z, Bruno Mars, Rhianna, etc.), I was especially astounded by what happened when Lady Gaga joined with Bradley Cooper (who hardly knew he can sing) and produced the soundtrack to *A Star is Born* and the song *Shallow* in particular. Lady Gaga (who writes her own music) has that rare direct connection to visceral creativity through music and they found a totally new outlet and channel of musical versatility together that moved millions of people to emotional highs on multiple levels. That is the extraordinary way that life channels creativity in the most unexpected yet inspiring ways that energizes and elevates collective consciousness. We all have personal preferences of course, but we should never utter a negative word about *any* music, even though we personally do not gravitate to that particular style or genre.

Movies

In this section of the book, we are discussing the Kundalini experience and how it manifested specifically in the physical body and now, how the presence and impact of this energy elevated the overall emotional constitution, specifically in terms of films. The point is that movies can nourish the passion toward life and, specifically, feed the aim of higher evolution. Movies have helped me on my journey as much as spirituality, art, and music, and I want to deliver exact details to make this point. A good part of the fun of engaging in such an inner jaunt toward a higher state of being is that this energy can appear in just about any form of entertainment.

The first movie that struck me in a deeper and more profound way than usual was *Rocky*, followed by *Rocky II*. This may come as a bit of a surprise because these weren't deep and profound movies with multiple levels of meaning and manifestations of Kundalini energy. I found that I closely identified with these stories of an underdog on one level and the enormous power of resurgence that pervades both movies. The energy of sheer determination and passion that drives Rocky is what *everybody* needs to empower their lives. It was largely the heartfelt love and emotional energy that captivated the audience. People felt a pitch of hope, drive, and redemption *in them-selves* as they rooted for Rocky to overcome the odds. This is an extremely important energy that we need to cultivate and feed; it is the fuel that drives survival. One scene in *Rocky II* remains, for me, one of the most emotionally potent moments I can remember on film. This, of course, is personal, and many may think it corny, but it is the moment after Rocky, who was determined to win his rematch against Apollo, was unable to focus on his training because his wife, Adrian, whom he loved deeply, was against him fighting for reasons concerning his health. For him, boxing was all he knew, but he was mentally distraught over Adrian's objection. Adrian knew her concern for his health was negatively affecting his mind and his training, and deep down she wanted to give him approval, but she couldn't in good conscience. As fate would have it, Adrian, who was nine months pregnant, fell ill and slipped into a coma. Rocky stopped all training and spent his time either by her bedside or at the hospital chapel praying for her, showing his deep love. Days later, Adrian awakens from the coma and sees Rocky's condition and how distraught and defeated he is. As they are holding their newborn baby for the first time, she sees how this entire ordeal has destroyed and beaten him down, which leads to the moment in the movie that I am referring to. Rocky tells her while she is still in her hospital bed that he is okay with not boxing anymore, but instead of Adrian agreeing and thanking him, she says, "There is one thing I want you to do for me ... Come here ... Win ... Win!"

At that moment, Apollo, his opponent, has no chance of winning, and everyone in the audience knows it. Rocky's body, emotion, and now mind lock into an unstoppable focus with overwhelming conviction and spirit. This was exactly the same inner dedication and devotion I felt toward my aim, and I actually used the "Overture" music written by Bill Conti from *Rocky II* hundreds of times to fuel my aim. The Kundalini energy is not obscure energy available only to acetic yogis in the mountains of the Himalayans; *it is in everything everywhere*. It is the spark, the drive, the electrical impulse that underlies all evolution. If we don't see it everywhere, including *Rocky* and just about everything else, then *we* are not looking – life's ultimate party includes everyone, everywhere, all the time.

Of course, it is important for me to note that the relevance between film and Kundalini is to show how, relative to conscious evolution and Kundalini, *everything* connects within the totality of our experience. For me, this particular movie supercharged my spirit, but for others, it may be something completely different. Not everyone will share my personal enjoyment of *Rocky*! The question is whether we are open inside to seeing more of what is before our very eyes and using it to nourish our souls.

There have been many other movies that inspired me that I have watched several times over because of the way they either uplifted my state or represented profound higher manifestations of energy. Key favorites are *Star Wars* and the entire concept of a Jedi, the Force, and the sheer cosmic power that can flow through humans from disciplined training. Yoda was always my personal idol. *Cocoon* and *The Green Mile* are two other films that communicated deep and profound messages. In both of these movies, there are supernatural higher energies that intercede with quite ordinary life circumstance—one in an old-age home and the other in a prison camp for criminals on death row. In *Cocoon*, aliens from another planet embody an irresistible energy that brings youthfulness, joy, sexual energy, and creativity to a group of elderly people in a nearby retirement home. In *The Green Mile*, one of my favorite characters in film, Koffee, is an enormously powerful and intimidating man who, by virtue of his innocence, is a channel of higher energies that work to overcome evil, protect life, and heal. He is on death row because he was caught trying to bring two children back to life after they were brutally murdered. Because he was black and had these two children in his hands when they were discovered, he was falsely accused, arrested, and given the death penalty without further investigation. Of course, the casting of Tom Hanks as the one person who connects to the supernatural energy couldn't have been more perfect. Both of these movies convey the mystical power of higher energy in the midst of everyday life. A few other movies that have esoteric themes embedded include Frank Capra's film *Lost Horizon, E.T.*, and *American Beauty*. From a specific point of view, we can see deeper themes in most movies if we look a certain way. What is even more enticing about all forms of entertainment is more profound than one might think. Art, music, and movies are creative expressions of life through humanity, and if we look closely and often, there is even more depth and beauty in these creations than we can account for. What this means is that by making a conscious effort to see how life communicates its beautiful intelligence through every creation, we can do our best to watch television, read books, and see movies *with this perspective in mind*. From this point of view, even Bugs Bunny can teach us how to awaken to a higher consciousness in the way he slyly outwits the lower level of intelligence of Elmer Fudd; or how our emotions are lifted when the Tin Man passionately strikes his ax into the door of the witch's castle to earn his heart by an act of sheer compassion and love of Dorothy. The idea is to raise our level of appreciation and discerning intelligence, so it is attuned to receiving higher frequencies of the greater intelligence of life, and spend our life growing to new heights. We must again remember that the wondrous creativity of life is behind all these creations and is outlandishly ingenious. When you consider your favorite movies, ask yourself what *you felt* inside while watching them. In a very real sense, you were high on inner energies. I would lastly recommend paying close attention to the scene in *American Beauty* referenced on the DVD version as "the most beautiful thing I ever filmed." In that scene, the character of Ricky shows his girlfriend, Jane, a fifteen-minute film he made of a plastic bag that is dancing in the wind, blowing about freely and inviting him to play and share in a magical moment with life. Ricky's consciousness was in a higher state of philosophic and transcendent stillness as he observed this otherwise mundane event and learned to never be afraid—*ever*—because life is ultimately a benevolent, wonderful energy, no matter what happens in the world of form and time. The artistic rendering of this scene oozes with high-powered insight mixed with deep gratitude and love of life. The director (Sam Mendes) added the perfect music for enough time to have a higher state sink into the audience, and focused on Ricky's face as he watches in wonder and mutters how he needs *to remember* this revelation. The idea of *remembering* is central to the aim of raising one's consciousness. We can read all the spiritual books ever written, but if we cannot remember and apply the wisdom, then we have not changed. These are all examples of how a movie can enrich our energy and how we process everyday life in a higher way.

Theater

There is a unique energy in theater in regard to this same theme of elevating oneself from the energy of entertainment. Early on, when I was quite young, two plays locked into my memory as profound and transformational. They were *Man of La Mancha* and *Pippin*. Later on in life, *Les Misérables* and others also had a lasting impact for similar reasons, but I will focus on these two as examples. It feels as if there is a certain vibration of energy when we enter a theater. It may have to do with the fact that there is a unique thrill to a live performance because it invites risk and the unknown. While this is true of all live events, including concerts and sports events, these particular plays struck me because they combined a meaningful message, emotional music, brilliant acting, and masterful staging. The overall impact of live theater is potent. When we see a play that we find entertaining (again, we all have different tastes), we are stimulated on a very high level from multiple sensory, intellectual, and emotional levels that foster this unique experience. While some people may have no attraction to musicals, that same person may have an interest in Shakespeare, comedy, or mysteries. The two plays I will briefly discuss are musicals whose music has lifted me for decades.

Man of La Mancha was a play that struck me psychologically and emotionally. The story was based on the classic book called *Don Quixote* by Miguel de Cervantes. The greatness of the story is in how a man, mired in books on chivalry, breaks from reality and imagines himself as a knight errant who is determined to right all wrongs and bring justice to the world (reflective of how higher consciousness works to undermine our own lower levels of consciousness). He is a lovable character whose innocence is irresistible as he charges windmills he takes as the enemy, enamors a prostitute he fancies as virtuous and beautiful, and takes all mundane things as things other than what they plainly are. It was the psychology reflected in this play that resonated with me as I was drawn to the process of discerning between *what is imagined and what is real*. Whether we as individuals can have a sense of humor when we realize that the vast majority of what goes through our minds is pure imagination and how we all have Don Quixote within us is key to higher states of consciousness. When we start laughing and enjoying the contents of our minds the way we enjoy a great character like Don Quixote, we have made dramatic progress in our own psychological evolution. In my case, I kept noticing how the thoughts in my head would constantly create stories about what was going on that were *simply not true*. You feel gas in your stomach, and the mind thinks you are having a heart attack. Or someone looks at you funny, and you spew hostilities, only to realize they are not wearing their glasses. Or a person doesn't return a text or email, and we feel hurt and rejected and engage in a defensive rant, only to find out they lost their phone the night before. How a projection can be completely baseless or how worry is almost always manufactured and virtually never happens can be a great source of awakening. It was this insight that freed me of so much mental mayhem in addition to the wonderful story of *Don Quixote*, which was then accentuated with triumphant music, that made this play unforgettable.

Pippin also delivered a strong psychological message with an inspiring soundtrack in finding one's *corner in the sky* or one's place in life. What I found psychologically compelling in this play was the struggle and search for meaning and significance and just how intense and passionate that search can be. This play features a main character, Pippin, who, in his search for meaning and purpose in life, is mentored charismatically by what is referred to as a *leading player*, similar to what I earlier referred to as a guide, that helps him come to realize that the search is not to be fulfilled by the outside world. Through great music and dance, this leading player accompanies Pippin through his journey until Pippin finally realizes for himself that there is no such thing as ever finding meaning and purpose in outer things, accomplishments, and material gain. That it is in the surrendering of that exhaustive search that one finds true fulfillment—a theme that life has parsed in most inspirational writing, spiritual scripture, and modern self-actualization psychology. The music again proved to be flawlessly aligned with the theatrics, and in this particular play, it is the addition of brilliant choreography and dance (by Bob Fosse) that deliver its message with excitement, celebration, and joy. Remember again that it is the total creativity of life that is behind all of this and most relevant to my purpose in this section.

These two examples, along with many other plays, deliver an extraordinary mode of creative expression that truly energizes us by combining the ingenuity of many different modes of expression, like writing, music, dance, staging, lighting, and set design. The impact on Kundalini energy is in feeding our emotions a high-energy food that helps sustain a positive state of mind. Appreciating such art and consciously using the messages and music is all part of one comprehensive awakening. Many times, I would turn to the music of the theater to reverse moods and break negative emotional patterns. Your favorites may be much different from my own, as we saw in movies and music, but that is the fun of it once again—*to find your own thread of elation through what excites you and enjoy the process along the way.* Everything you love *is your own thread*, and connecting them is and should be your personal work of living art.

Humor

I talked about laughter in the section on the physical Kundalini experiences and how laughter, in my journey, became directly connected to higher states of being. I spoke of uncontrollable hysterics and a laughing gas high that feels like a natural drug produced in the body. Everybody laughs—and we should all laugh more often and much harder when we do. It has a powerful healing effect emotionally and physically. The world of comedy and humor—like music, art, and movies—has played a big role in my journey. Personally, due to the current leadership and political atmosphere circa 2017, I've made it a point to watch at least ten to fifteen minutes of *Seinfeld* just before I fall asleep. My wife and kids joke about how I can relate just about anything in life to *Seinfeld* and Larry David's *Curb Your Enthusiasm*. Comedy breaks life's hypnotic hold on us, and there is not a human being alive who does not welcome laughter when it comes. The unexpected, which is a major part of comedy, is something that life itself enjoys to break up the boredom and repetition. Stand-up comedians deliver an artform that I hold dear, and, as surprising as it may sound, comedians are very close cousins to spiritual teachers. I distinctly remember Dr. Sohn, the teacher who founded the Institute for Self-Development, where this all started for me, said that he had to decide whether to become a spiritual teacher or a stand-up comedian. The main reason for this is that comedians are astute observers of life and have the uncanny ability to deliver those observations in a context that we can relate to. We laugh because we recognize the similarity in our own lives. Stand-up comedians are ingenious in their style, their timing, their facial expressions, and their total delivery. Think of George Carlin, Richard Pryor, Eddie Murphy, Robin Williams, and on and on, and we see this spectacular art in full expression. A powerful influence on my spiritual journey came from one of the most controversial and prolific spiritual teachers, Bhagwan Rashneesh (1931–1980), later known as OSHO. He had the gift of being hilarious while he delivered deep esoteric interpretations and talks on just about every spiritual tradition in history. There is no way not to enjoy laughter, although we certainly do not share in agreeing on what is funny and what is not. What is essential is to make sure laughter is a big part of our lives, because it is most certainly connected to higher energies and, at the very least, is a healthy way to live and an immediate relief from stress. A key antidote to being overly serious is to simply have fun and alter our own body chemistry for its own benefit by laughing, giggling, and joking in the privacy of our own minds. There is a great benefit to be derived from pondering the entire existence of humor, laughter, and comedy in all its forms. Breaking the hypnosis of the seriousness of life is liberating and freeing. Humanity becomes deadly serious, which cannot be helped in times of terror and grief, but it must be tempered with smiles, giggles, and downright belly laughs. Only then can we see clearly and plainly. A direct example of this connection between laughter and higher consciousness can be enjoyed in certain talks by Eckhart Tolle. If you are a follower of his teaching and have experienced a talk live or on video, he sometimes becomes filled with spontaneous laughter while amid a talk. One can see the giddiness and joy bubble up in him. His face lights up, and he goes into a state of laughter in midsentence; the audience often joins in on this laughter when this happens. It is all part of higher being sharing a higher state of being *together*—a very powerful manifestation of the creativity of life itself celebrating its own creation. We should all find our favorite humor and bask it in often.

Relationships

Everything we've shared in this section has been about enhancing the energy of emotion through various mediums. Without question, there are levels of emotion felt by all, but we rarely differentiate the actual quality of the inner experiences, remember them, and intentionally and consciously increase their frequency and intensity which is where we want to be. The world of relationships promises potential for the growth of consciousness but is certainly the most dynamic and difficult way to grow. While art, music, nature, spirituality, and entertainment engage external things and activities, relationships are a constant interplay of forces based on moods, temperaments, hormones, changing circumstances, and a host of other factors. We can feel intense love one moment and deep rage and anger toward that same person a split second later. Most of the poetry about love centers on forgiveness, empathy, and service to others, while we are naturally selfish and viscerally defensive. It makes for quite a challenge and endless inner conflict. The energy of consciousness and Kundalini fuels a drive to encompass our total emotional constitution, which is incessantly swinging back and forth between opposites. Higher consciousness evolves around an inner taste for unconditional love, and from it, we learn to naturally resist all forms of negative emotions. If earnestly pursued (or gifted to enlightenment by birth), a dramatic insight and transformation can occur relative to emotions that cannot be described, only experienced. This extraordinary evolution involves a state of being that is liberated from space and time altogether and leaves one in a state of pure, undisturbed bliss. However, most of us find ourselves continually in the torrent of uninvited negative emotions. The lower emotions of fear, hostility, and sadness are lightning fast and can overtake our entire being in the blink of the eye. What offers hope is that an even faster and more ingenious level of consciousness, backed by a drive to overcome these lower emotions, can be realized with attentive effort. In the Work I studied, much time was spent observing and pondering the nature of emotions and how the only form of higher emotions was those with no opposite and where life is no longer paradoxical. Think about what it means for an emotion to have no opposite; it means it would not swing back and forth like a pendulum, which is the cause of most of our suffering. Although we will explore the transformation that the intellect brings to the process, it is always the sheer drive of emotion that *fuels* change. For me, without a deep love for life, nature, and people, I don't know how I would have continued with this inner struggle. Perhaps the most transformational emotions regarding relationships are grief and loss. No other emotions raise our level of awareness and attention the way *loss* does, and loss can include losing anything we love and value— even things like our youth, the initial passion in a relationship, *or our hair*. When filled with this painful emotion, our bodies suffer, and our mind is gripped and locked into a form of hypnosis. Words are weak and largely powerless as people do their best to console us, but it is as if our emotions are in a different dimension, and worse yet, we feel alone because no one is actually experiencing our grief exactly as we do. It is only by learning to channel emotions toward one singular aim of inner growth that we have any hope of bringing meaning to these experiences. There are many spiritual teachings that suggest that an aspirant of higher consciousness is best served by viewing all his or her personal challenges as necessary for personal evolution. The more we fight and resist what happens in our lives, the more we suffer; but when we welcome, encompass, and allow our feelings to be without judgment, we are free to explore new possibilities. What I came to understand over time in regard to emotion is that we can't stop them or intellectually circumvent them. They have to play out almost like the flu. No matter how physically healthy we may be, we cannot convince our body not to have a fever, chills, and the aches and pains of an actual flu. We can certainly diffuse the intensity of negative emotions and substantially weaken their sting, but to think we can be liberated and free of emotion is virtually impossible unless a totally new state of consciousness arises, which has only been realized by the most unusual human beings in our history—the enlightened. I found that virtually the only way to really battle a stressful state is to take the challenge by the throat and confront it head-on: call the person who is stressing you, get out of bed and turn the lights on if you are worrying incessantly, move out of your home if you find it hopelessly lonely. I hope this book offers tantalizing insight into how to work on emotion *creatively*. Relationships can pose the greatest challenge and offer the most opportunity to work on them. The last point I will make on using relationships to foster higher consciousness is that it challenges us to venture beyond ourselves and into the experience of another person. We naturally live within the confines of our own experiential realm. It becomes a habit that we cannot even see, which is why we tend to suffer over the exact same thing over and over. To travel consciously into the actual experience of another person takes listening without the mayhem and cacophony of your own mental history—which takes work. Most of our consciousness and energy is drained not by the actual events in our lives but by the words that pass automatically in our minds *about* those events. Think about this. If you see the truth of this, it could startle you. Do we fear monsters or the word "monster"? Especially since there is no such things as monsters.

The Intellect's Expansion

Higher Consciousness and Kundalini Energy

My hope in this section is to convey the role that the intellect played as this spiritual search merged with Kundalini activity and ran the course I am retracing. This is challenging because I explored many different teachers and teachings and seamlessly assimilated them into my experience over decades without communicating it to others. As you know by now, I delved into these teachings on my own and pursued this direction without once thinking I would recount the story or try to convey it publicly. This search and exploration continue to this day, as I will cover some of the most profitable and potent ideas in terms of this intellectual pursuit.

In order to make this as clear and concise as possible, I decided to deliver the central ideas in the same chronological order I experienced them to help lend direction and cohesiveness. Much of what I'm about to share is pure psychological insight that can be easily argued as having nothing to do with Kundalini. I neither disagree nor object to that observation. *The point I am making is that everything connects within the context as a whole.* Kundalini furnishes energy and creativity that our organism can produce to drive toward a higher state of being. Think of your own energy that desires to read and (hopefully) finish this book; it is *that energy* that can evolve into a higher form, which is what Kundalini is potentially about. Kundalini activation can be considered a mysterious potential that supercharges that very evolution. It is the underlying energy in everyone who is reverberating with a search for something higher. When a certain quantity of energy is available in the brain and is unencumbered by the fetters of attachments, neurosis, distraction, and disorder, it tends to expand with new observations, realizations, and revelations. As I trace these ideas, there will be some reiterations that I have briefly referenced earlier, but, due to their importance and a slight embellishment, I felt it necessary to include. Here are the ideas with accompanying commentary.

A Key Principle of Growth via Self-Actualization and Peak Experiences

Earlier I noted that my first interest in psychology was in the work of Abraham Maslow and his concept of self-actualization. The core principle of his idea is that as one adequately addresses one's needs for food, water, and shelter; higher needs, *or meta-needs*, as he called them, are free to seek fulfillment. Examples of meta-needs are truth, beauty, justice, meaningfulness, self-transcendence, and creative expression. In essence, a person who satisfies their needs for food, safety, and belongingness ventures into the higher needs of self-esteem and ultimately self-actualization. A clear example of this is that a starving person or one who does not have a stable living environment will be hard-pressed to adore the beauty of dolphins and eagles. At the more advanced levels, if we are entangled in our troubled self-esteem, hostility toward others, and unrealistic, childish demands, we will not be exploring the *Higher Reaches of Human Nature*, which is the title of one of Maslow's cornerstone books. This is a key principle of growth and one of the best models that we can apply to ourselves. The enduring question is whether *we* have a discerning awareness of where *we* stand relative to our own growth. Many of us get to a certain point in life and anticipate and expect good things to happen because we feel we are entitled to it. The blunt answer to this idea is that we are not entitled to anything. If we do not take responsibility for our growth, then we are no better than a pathetic gambler depending on luck to make money, which is a big mistake. While we are all far from perfect and will repeat ourselves ad nauseam, a part of our consciousness needs to tend to our bodies, emotions, and minds like a gardener tends a garden. Without incessant (moment to moment and day to day) pruning, removing weeds, and tilling the soil, we cannot expect healthy crops (a healthy mind). Although this is cliché and simple wisdom, in order to expect a higher experience, we need to be responsible for the basic principles of a sound body and a peaceful mind. The question is whether we have a conscientious plan in place to achieve such, and more importantly, whether we execute the plan (as opposed to perseverating about it recklessly).

As an adjunct to the idea of self-actualization, Maslow introduced another pertinent idea to the higher spectrum of human experience that he named *peak experiences*, and later, *plateau experiences*. These are the most powerful and positive experiences that are evoked in us, during which there is a biological rush of higher energy that storms from within and manifests as pure joy. Many people have these extraordinary experiences, although they are infrequent and short-lived. I purposely added the word "biological" because I feel that plateau experiences are that higher energy (Kundalini) that secretly and silently is interlaced into everyday life without our notice. Peak experiences are those moments when everything is clicking, good things are converging, and optimism is exploding uncontrollably. They evoke a timeless state of being when we want to almost cry about the way life is crystal perfect at that extraordinary moment. What differentiates these experiences from simple emotional highs is that they are fully and completely self-fulfilling. *A true peak experience does not need to be communicated to others;* it is its own reward and therefore uniquely valuable to one who is working on oneself. We learn from experience that most attempts to communicate such transformational moments are often met with a discouraging lack of interest—and for good reason; *the person who is hearing about your wonderful moment is not in an elevated state of their own while they are hearing it.* They are simply hearing words minus the intense emotion. The image of Rocky on top of the steps pumping his fists with his music blasting in unison was always, for me, a great external representation of moments like these, but when working on yourself, they occur internally and without an audience. These experiences come in just about any form at any time and are highly individualistic. That energy must be garnered, remembered, repeated, and—most of all—*celebrated.* As we shall see later, consciousness longs to interlink higher experiences and form into a new dimension of experience with which to embrace life. These higher experiences are supremely healthy and offer a much-needed electrical boost to our daily lives. The more we align ourselves with life, the more these experiences occur, and the more they occur, the more we attract circumstances that encourage them to occur more. These are the experiences that initially opened my consciousness to higher states and prepared me for what was to come through Kundalini. It is also important to note that the prior section that outlined a powerful emotional experience relative to the creative arts is a prime source for such extraordinary experiences. It is important to remain connected to those highs we receive when we are immersed in spirituality, music, art, and so

95

on. Remember that this is all connected, and it is the fabric of our own experiences that can and will help us grow. It is important that this does not become and remain philosophy. Think of the highs in your life and the energy they deliver to you. Consider and remember moments when you personally were most elated, excited, and filled with joy. That energy must become conscious. What I mean by "become conscious" is that there is much more to what I am saying than becoming a junkie of conditional, momentary surface happiness. While there is nothing wrong with these states, and I experience them from music, laughter, and nature all the time, it is the timeless joy *beyond* the experience that is far more inviting. Extreme ups and downs are not what we are after; that we can get from a roller coaster. We want to *be* an amusement park like AstroWorld, not be one particular ride, and we want to enjoy the park and not depend on whether one particular ride is open that day. If our happiness depends on external events, we are doomed. The question is whether we can build an inner constitution that sustains peace and contentment despite external events. One last point is that one does not have to be experiencing explosive jubilation for it to be a peak experience. They are often your highest quality private moments involving music, a book, nature, or any of your most valued experiences that are known only to your-self. Are you conscious of your most fulfilling moments in this life?

Cosmological Perspective and Creating Inner Distance from Ordinary Thought

The transformational idea that followed quickly and complemented self-actualization for me was the wave of revelations that were inspired by Carl Sagan that grew into what I called a cosmological perspective. As referenced earlier, Sagan poetically articulated the wonder of the universe while scientifically delivering the startling details of the cosmos that otherwise might bore some of us. My consciousness was captivated by the grand design but focused on the implications on our psychology. I remember experiencing a distinct sense of our smallness and mortality considering the infinite space and prodigious time periods he communicated. I remember the existential impact this had on my ego and self-righteous indignation that our wonderful, miraculous planet was less than a speck in the universe, was by no means at the center of anything, and our species was metaphorically in its infancy in the context of cosmic time. It was shocking and enabled my consciousness to create an invaluable distance from thought and emotion. When aware of our existential place in space and time, it becomes more difficult to take things too seriously. Remembering these ideas in real time is what conscious evolution is about. We all *know* these things, but we hardly *remember* them when being cut off on the road or in the throes of anger about some transitory event that we forget seconds later.

This cosmological perspective expanded greatly as I studied the ideas of George Gurdjieff and Jan Cox. Gurdjieff delivered an extraordinary perspective that clearly indicated that humanity finds itself amid an enormous cosmos, and his role must be to awaken and ascend what he called the "ray of creation." According to this model, a person seeking to awaken does so by doing inner work on oneself to become more conscious. The entirety of his teachings was based on deliberate efforts to free oneself from the monotonous, hypnotic spell that humanity is engulfed in, which he referenced as being asleep. Becoming more awake for a human would mean becoming increasingly more conscious and responsible for the self. The Gurdjieff work is powerful and complex. I wouldn't begin to attempt to divulge his teachings, but I wanted to stress how important a cosmological perspective is in the context of work on oneself. *Without a higher perspective, it's nearly impossible to transform oneself.* The analogy often given is that it is like trying to move a plank of wood you are standing on. We, our consciousness, needs to experience and sense space between our sentient awareness and the thoughts that play in our heads. We need to *watch* a worry pass like a white puffy cloud against a blue sky. *How am I going to support myself? Is there something wrong with my health? Does my partner want to stay with me?* If we are fully immersed in such thoughts, without creating an inner distance and objectivity, then we suffer under their spell. We must establish a sacred inner space we call home, and a cosmological perspective helps furnish the energy needed to establish this much-needed space.

Jan Cox imparted a perspective that influenced many of the ideas in this book and most especially this idea of using a cosmological perspective that greatly impacted my relationship to thought. One of his key ideas that I consider cosmological is that life itself is an alive, living, and growing organism in which everything is necessary, nothing is wasted, and the aim is to expand and become more complex (which comes via simplicity). Comprehending that we are part of a much larger living being helps explain many phenomena that otherwise appear as blatantly absurd. Life certainly is not a perfected masterpiece that is static and without change. On the contrary, it is movement, change, and evolution. Life is a living process, and only the lower mind perceives it in static fragments and insists on believing that is all there is. This leads to disappointment and frustration. A view that life itself is alive and growing helps our individual mind embrace new insights and potential to expand on that perspective. Altering our perception from still-frame photography to a living, moving video is not only more enjoyable but also rich with insight. To connect this idea to the previous idea, our thoughts again become phenomena to be observed and transcended because they are part of a process. They are not complete and final realities. Thoughts often vanish simply by poking a person. Or simply throw a ball at them and watch the thoughts scatter off for at least a few moments until the person can *remember* to worry again. Quickly realize that one actually does have to *remember* to think or worry about something. If we couldn't remember to worry about something (past or future) we would be in the proverbial NOW or a state of enlightenment.

In the next subsection, I'll outline in more detail the specific impact these cosmological perspectives have on the way we process experience, events, and our inner emotional and mental states. For now, the point is that we need to move outside of time, ponder the existence we find ourselves in, and remain in awe of the wonder of it all. Immersing ourselves in larger cosmological ideas creates this cherished distance we long for. We ought to disturb the grip of thought. Most of us live under a hypnotic spell, believing our stream of thoughts are absolute reality and that there are no other options. There are millions of other options, which is what the idea of awakening is all about. Like being high on a mind-altering drug, the person is flabbergasted by what is possible outside the confines of their routine thinking. The problem is that people who are dependent on the drug cannot stay in that desired place and seek more drugs to go back there. This is not transformational psychology; that is drug addiction. I strongly urge anyone who is intrigued with the idea of transcending thought to open up to Eckhart Tolle's ideas in the book, A New Earth and the next stage of human evolution.

Conscious Reflection

Earlier in the book, I described the practice of pondering. If we recall, it was in the context that, for our consciousness to increase and expand, we must practice observing and looking, but more importantly, thinking openly and creatively about what we are seeing. Because I was exposed to the idea of self-actualization, followed by a cosmological perspective, I couldn't help but think about how everything connected. When we are moved by something, when something stirs us deep within, we can't help but raise our eyes up to the sky and wonder. Many of us do this without noticing what a profound act it is for our brain to automatically start ruminating about something we have just heard or learned. It is as though life itself is thinking about its own creation *through us*. It is second nature for us to converse spontaneously, exchange opinions and beliefs, all while talking faster than we can think. This is all quite extraordinary. When we are alone, we are more apt to reflect in a more personal manner on our experience because we have full access to everything that is going on in our lives without the pressure and anxiety of worrying about how others might interpret what we say or think. In this private inner place, there is a specific thread of thought that seeks to understand a particular nuance about us or the world. Conscious reflection is that singular inner drive that is seeking to link things together in a way that delivers realizations that enlighten and improve our lives. The less entangled our minds are in neurosis, paranoid fears, and hostility toward others, the more we want to explore how we can interconnect our higher experiences into a new way of processing life. In terms of these higher energies, and Kundalini in particular, not only is it more profitable to free oneself from the toxins of lower emotions, but it is incredibly more enjoyable, fun, and enlivening to openly think, reflect, and ponder about the life we are living. The key is to have a goal so that all such reflection is driving toward that end, as opposed to random disconnected observations. A cosmological perspective helps keep us from spiraling too far into negative self-absorption and also serves as a reminder to use our life to evolve toward higher consciousness. Such practices and efforts can lead to new ways of processing life experiences, as we will see in the following pages. Most importantly, we are encouraged to rhetorically ask ourselves whether we have a well-thought-out process of evaluating our behaviors, emotions, and thoughts in the context of growth. Are we positioned to take whatever life offers as an opportunity to learn, expand, include, and transcend? If not, we are robotic victims of circumstances, and life can become a tedious chore and a dreadful disappointment. Our spirits need to feel fascinated and excited about uncovering parts of ourselves so we can open up to new possibilities. For me, without having the internal distance of a cosmological perspective, it would be impossible to have leverage over the lower and less evolved states of myself that allowed me to open into this unpredictable journey into uncharted inner territory. In my personal life, the practice of long walks, keeping a journal, and maintaining a balance of living and learning simultaneously served to enrich this experience. My dual life largely took root from this particular enjoyment of exploring quietly while simultaneously living life. It was as if I was talking to life about *itself*. This practice was self-fulfilling and complete—until now. What I have noticed lately is that while many people enjoy talking and opening up to how wondrous life is, people also, quite naturally and spontaneously, feel invigorated when they start talking about *how they feel, think, and behave*. Everybody apparently is observing, pondering, and thinking about their internal life but often keeps it hidden and in the recesses of their private mind. This, of course, is not a new revelation and is the basis of the value of having a good friend we can confide in or a therapist, or reading a book that opens doors to ourselves. What I am emphasizing is making that process a more benevolent, pleasant, and ever-growing creative dimension of one's inner life. In other words, talk to yourself about yourself so you keep learning, laughing, and adding to your own self-understanding. The key is to not be an enemy to yourself but your own best friend. Your personal life is your home, and it is critical to our sanity to enjoy being home. Remember, "There is no place like home."

High-Speed Intelligence and New Mental Processing

Far along this journey, many seekers pose the following questions:

"What, after all this work and effort, has actually changed in me?"

"How am I different today than before I embarked on this journey?"

"If I am more conscious, how so?"

While the sheer involvement in such a journey has changed our lives, it does not necessarily mean that *we* have changed. Many of us have in some way altered our diets to be healthier, read books that opened our minds, connected with one or many teachers of higher consciousness, practiced meditation or yoga, and participated in one or more of these practices that pleasantly have led to a better, more joyful and peaceful life. We can easily say that the payoff is this new and better life and we are happier because of it. This is all, of course, true. Any person who has searched and found a new dimension they deem spiritual, healthier, and more self-fulfilling contends that they are far better off than before and are grateful for this new and improved life. But there is a deeper take on this same question that is more compelling: *has this inner work or practice produced a change in the way we process and experience life?*

In other words, if we don't respond to ordinary events differently from before, if we repeat the same patterns of suffering from the same internal agony, then how are we different? More bluntly, if a bodybuilder goes to a gym for three years, he or she can most certainly measure progress by either comparing the changes in muscle mass or by lifting more weight than previously. The change is palpable and observable. Work on one's inner psychology cannot be quantified in the same way because it is subjective. If we do not periodically cross-examine ourselves with uncritical self-observation, then we may be deluding ourselves into believing that the act of reading, attending lectures, and meditating is actually changing us, when it may not have changed us much at all. Most of us are quietly troubled by the fact that, even after so much apparent self-work, we stay relatively the same. We have experiences, mostly in the privacy of our own minds, where we say or think, *I'm still exactly as I was before!* This is disturbing because it rubs our ego negatively and discourages our efforts. For me personally, this question is probably the single most relevant question we can ask ourselves and one that has spawned several distinct responses that encouraged me in my own work.

The first revelation I had when I observed myself relative to this question was that, while most of my reactions to the outside world were similar if not identical, the reactions *did not last and linger as long as they did before*. Whether involved in a disappointment at work, such as losing to a competitor, or a hostile defensive reaction to a family member, or the immediate paranoia associated with a health issue—all such reactions had significantly less duration. Clear and rational thinking displaces the suffering, and I don't spend hours or days in a reaction but rather more like minutes and seconds, although this could vary based on the severity of the situation. The duration of time we spend engaged in an extreme of any type, even happiness, is important to notice, because it means we are conscious of it.

As the duration of time in reactive states diminished, I also observed that the intensity of an emotional reaction had lessened significantly. While it is true that we biochemically change as we get older, and we should keep this in mind, my emotional reactions did not have the same overwhelming effect they had prior to advanced self-observation. It felt as if my consciousness, over time, had become more prevalent, which diffused the potency and degree of my internal and external reactions to those events. This ties directly to the internal distance I spoke of earlier that was the result of moving toward a cosmological perspective. As a situation would unfold, a higher state of consciousness served more as a witness and less as a participant. It was as if a different partition in the brain was watching the event and the reaction to the event in slow motion. Prior to this stage, I would have been swept up into an extreme reaction and so totally identified with it that it wouldn't dawn on me that there was an alternative response. By virtue of having an aim, developing a cosmological perspective, and having a repository of observations over time, the intensity of the reaction became impotent and weak. The entire process of handling perceptions of external events proactively and consciously generated significantly more energy so I could pursue higher mental processes.

As I conserved energy by suffering less and fed higher emotions in the ways expressed earlier through music, people, and art, and as the Kundalini energy provided powerful surges of electrical currents that encouraged the process further, new mental processes formed that I believe hastened my inner growth. These new psychological processes served one intention—*to outwit suffering through more advanced levels of awareness.* I had come to a place where I couldn't bear the experience of negative emotions and undisciplined thoughts that served no purpose other than to make everything worse. Physical pain from my body was unavoidable, and I needed to accept this part of life, but staying angry over an occurrence that happened hours or seconds ago seemed intolerable. In the Gurdjieff work, this was called having "inner taste." Feeling my own toxic emotions became like tasting sour milk. We are internally tasting our own foul behavior relative to our intention. Jan Cox had a similar experience of being disgusted by his own manifest behavior in that, after saying or thinking something he regretted (split seconds after it spewed out), he described feeling as if he had "caterpillars crawling on his tongue"—a most effective image and accurate conveyance of what this feels like! In both examples, the necessary ingredient is getting to a place where we want to act on our own inner values as opposed to wishing, praying, or hoping we might change. The compulsion to act on an observation compels new growth opportunities. Taking responsibility for one's own inner (and thus, outer) states becomes second nature.

These changes in mental processing led to some of the most profound new ways that my consciousness began to operate and approach information. What follows is challenging to express, but the point I want to make is well worth the effort. Consider the way computers today are designed to process multiple levels of data simultaneously. Consider the fact that the microprocessor *itself* is operating on a higher level in order to process the graphics and programs of today's software. Now consider how our consciousness (which actually created microprocessors to begin with) can also be wired to process multiple data streams of information to help us transform experience and changes in our lives. Specifically, consider how our consciousness can access memories, insights, and learned wisdom while receiving bad news, or even good news for that matter. A new arrangement of our own intelligence would entertain multiple possibilities, run them against past experiences, and consider images from self-observation—*all at the same time.* The processing is fast, efficient, and pointed. The aim is to reduce suffering by cornering the lower, less intelligent parts of ourselves and replacing them with new neural pathways—like moving from old-fashioned locomotives to high-speed monorails or routing data through a modern high-speed fiber network as opposed to cumbersome mainframe computers. All this is done under the context of the goal to increase one's conscious evolution. We know that our brains already perform these functions naturally. To clearly articulate exactly what I am referring to, I'm going to provide three specific practices, two of which are applied concepts from Gurdjieff and Jan Cox, and a third that is a practice I developed as a result of my own applied efforts. As you read what follows, keep in mind that some of the practices formed and emerged after years of work on myself. Give these ideas time to seep in and become part of your understanding.

1. Advanced Self-Observation and Neural Recordings and Mental Photography

In the psychological work of Gurdjieff, there is an emphasis on self-observation that we have touched on several times. To observe oneself sounds straightforward, easy to grasp, and quite familiar. At the beginning of this practice, the basic results are that we slowly become more aware of what we *are*—without filters, stories, or imagination. Most people carry a more or less vague sense of themselves, without stark detail. In general, people speak of themselves in terms like being lazy, angry, nervous, sad, relatively happy, cynical, pessimistic, and so on. We often might explain ourselves (if asked) in the following ways: *I like to work out, I enjoy movies, I read a lot of books, I don't like politics, I dislike being alone, I can't handle stress …* We tend to live our lives carrying our baggage through the vicissitudes of life with periodic intervals of self-reflection but do not engage in a disciplined and comprehensive exploration of ourselves. The exception are those people who are either naturally introspective or have a therapist to help them better understand themselves. Let's recall the fact that most people do not have a need to delve into their inner psyche because they feel they are just fine as they are—and they are largely correct (for themselves). Most people enjoy their lives and welcome the spice that their hostilities add to the everyday events that occur. Most people are not seeking to be silent monks who eat rice and listen to gongs or raindrops splattering on a tree. Many people enjoy simply kicking ass, or else life would be boring. Historically, it has always been a relatively small subset of people, or *the few*, that many spiritual teachers aim to teach. These students or aspirants have a ravenous appetite to expand themselves into uncharted frontiers of their own being, which makes them different from ordinary people. This is simple to grasp. It is really no different from comparing ourselves to a marathon runner. As much as we might like to be healthy, we might not have any inclination to run those extraordinary distances. Just so, most people will not feel that it is necessary to undergo the rigors of self-observation. Keep this in mind as you read what follows regarding advanced self-observation and what I mean by neural recordings and mental photography. Without a clear aim to mobilize higher energies within us, such efforts as I will describe could sound unnecessary or laborious. Also bear in mind that if done more or less correctly, such practice creates a new, enjoyable, and jovial inner relationship to yourself and never a hostile angry world of self-hate and self-loathing. To convey this concept and purpose of neural recording and mental photography, consider this idea:

> *If a lawyer had to plead a case, they would present evidence that would seek to prove, beyond a shadow of a doubt, that the plaintiff was guilty. The best possible evidence is an actual picture or video of the accused performing the act on camera. Providing the images and videos are authentic, a picture of the accused firing a gun at the now deceased murder victim with a bullet in the exact spot of the coroner report would shut the case with no further deliberation.*

In terms of the above idea, a person seeking to become liberated longs to stop all superfluous mental narratives and needs to prove without a shadow of a doubt that the mind is engaged in defending lies, partial truths, and false pictures of oneself and ego. It is to this end that advanced self-observation evolves into these ideas I am discussing. The higher consciousness in us records mental word tracks and takes inner photographs and video of ourselves *caught in the act* of being contrary to the valued pictures we hold of ourselves. These recordings, pictures, and video are then stored in a special form of memory and used to dissolve self-delusion. In other words, you fancy yourself to be a warm, kindhearted person, yet this inner paparazzi starts presenting uncontestable photos of you acting out in the world as coldhearted and selfish. By photo, I literally mean a picture or image (albeit in the mind's eye). When confronted with such an actual mental picture, it becomes increasingly impossible to imagine yourself as a reincarnation of Gandhi. The behavior is in the spotlight of your own consciousness, and there is no further deliberation.

Here are three personal examples of how increasing consciousness with this practice has helped me encompass more of my true nature and diffuse pent-up tension, defensiveness, and self-righteousness. The aim is always to promote an inner atmosphere that is open, free, and unfettered, to break apart the automatic trance of what we mechanically are.

- At my job, I am looked upon as being well composed, rarely stressed, and unperturbed by failure. Yet I have clear and direct accounts of myself feeling distraught, anxious, and unable to stop anxiety in the form of worry and exaggerated negative self-talk. My consciousness has stored many inner snapshots and videos of me immersed in these states that blatantly contradict this image and picture of myself as cool and composed.

- In relation to people, my persona gives off an air of aplomb or self-assured levelheadedness, of not being angry, violent, or competitive. Yet I have personally collected many examples, again in the form of actual mental pictures, of me being angry and malicious and wishing others would fail so that I can feel good about myself. I distinctly observed my mind lashing out, criticizing, and feeling a perverse satisfaction when someone did not win the lottery (so to speak). My ego is as petty, childish, and imbecilic as anyone could be (I am not saying that yours is, just my own).

- To myself, and as evidenced largely in this book, I have experienced many positive emotions, elation, wonder, rapture, and so on. I have good reason to believe and uphold a picture of myself of not being depressed or cynical, and the people who know me would agree that they rarely if ever have seen me overtly down or verbalizing negativity. Yet again, my consciousness is well aware, through direct self-observation and neural photography, that my inner raw reactions to life are outraged by the apparent injustices in life. I have directly observed an ongoing simmering agitation toward certain people and find myself distressed if not depressed by how seemingly impossible it is for the good in life to overcome evil.

Having worked on these psychological practices for many years, I have a full storehouse of such images contradicting most of these ridiculous pictures of myself I held dear. In the Gurdjieff system, this was called "Work Memory," which was articulated with precision by his student Maurice Nicoll in his series of books called the *Commentaries on the Teachings of Gurdjieff and Ouspensky.* Work Memory is a special memory of these recordings, pictures, and videos that one uses to temper and balance one's own psychology. In the school I attended, we were tasked to write a log of such observations and record everything from the physical posture and positions of our bodies to the range of emotional states that manifested during the event, as well as the thoughts that appeared in our heads (the accompanying narrative). This makes for quite a detailed level of self-awareness that helps reduce how much we identify with the ego or *pain body*, which is Eckhart Tolle's term. The principle is that when we are conscious of these otherwise unconscious aspects of ourselves, it tends to weaken their hold on us considerably. These efforts were meant to create new energy that could be used to channel toward a further unknown level of being and processing of life. Believe it or not, such practices lead to quite an astounding revelation—*that everything I am saying actually vanishes, leaving you free and purely self-aware*, but we will not go there just yet.

2. Neuralizing—A Jan Cox Idea Applied to a New Circuit in Humanity

Jan Cox invented a term he called *neuralizing.* The word was derived by combining "neural" and "neutral," and it is a process of consciously interrupting mechanical conditioned reactions by *not* immediately reacting with one's full genetic temperament to everyday events and circumstances. It is a method whereby the practitioner floats their awareness above the polarized reactions they would normally have, thereby creating new energy and therefore a new opportunity to grow (one that did not exist before), in order to expand consciousness. It is a variation on the idea of nonidentification with one's thoughts or emotions. To remain on point, let's recall that this section is about new ways of processing life experiences, with the aim of transcending our ordinary selves. The key objective is to suffer less, increase energy, and expand our consciousness into new areas and frontiers by seeing, encompassing, and connecting more information together about ourselves and the world around us. Jan referred to this idea as building a new circuit within human consciousness (a similar refrain of Eckhart's new stage of human evolution that encompasses and goes beyond thought through stillness). We need to recall and remember that such a change in processing requires enough psychological interest in exploring new ways to experience life, or else such a concept like this will sound ludicrous and unnecessary at best. In other words, if we are happy as we are, we will not seek to alter ourselves for the better. The idea of neuralizing can take time to grasp, largely because it is more about *seeing* and less about intellectually understanding, but that is the fun of it. If we are not enjoying the process of self-evolution, we will not realize its full benefits. Jan defines neuralizing as the practice of *thinking about something without remembering it*, or in reverse, *remembering something without thinking about it*. This might sound odd, and it is. Let those words sink in without trying to intellectually grasp it. To accurately convey this idea, I am going to create a hypothetical example from ordinary life, which will serve to force mimic the mental process that will help me explain how neuralizing works and how it can be applied to ourselves to expand growth. The example might sound extreme, but it is purposeful for the sake of making the point:

> *Imagine you are out and about walking, and suddenly you receive a text that someone you love dearly was just taken to the hospital and is not responding … Virtually a second later, as you are starting to react emotionally to the text, a car veers out of control and right at you! You spin away and leap to the side of the road, where you tumble down a small embankment. You are now in a mild state of shock but safe. The physical shock to your body is all that is experienced for the next few seconds as your mind then starts firing obscenities of angry blame and outrage toward the driver that almost hit you. Slowly you get up as the driver rushes to see if you are all right and quickly*

explains that she is an animal lover and swerved away from hitting a squirrel and lost control. You then start coming back to yourself and realize you are not harmed. You forgive the innocent driver, and, at that point, the memory of your loved one on the way to the hospital returns to your consciousness (in other words, you remember to worry about it).

I understand that this is a harrowing example, but as I said earlier, it is purposeful. Remember that this was all made up, and I will extrapolate what is meant by neuralizing from the mental processing that took place in the mind of this individual.

Now consider what happened psychologically. This fictitious person was just about to start reacting to the sudden bad news in a typical, predictable, conditioned fashion (in other words, suffer), and rightfully so. Anyone of us would instantly feel sad, frightened, nervous, and perhaps start crying upon hearing such news. But this particular person's body was thrown into trauma virtually simultaneously, which physiologically took precedence over the emotional reaction, and as a result, the normal mental narrative could not play out in its conditioned manner. Before the quick brush with death, he would have become quite emotional and steeped in a negative mental narrative. *In this example though, this person could not think about the bad news that had just been processed.* He could not process it normally because of the shock to his overall being. From the perspective of Jan's concept of neuralizing, the person could not "think about it." The words and thoughts could not play out. During those few lightning-fast seconds, those thoughts could not air in his mind the way they normally would have, which is key to the aim of reducing the suffering that normally goes on in our minds. The question is, can we use our consciousness to avert the ordinary scripted narratives that plague, torment, and engulf us in everyday life? Can we use our very own personal attention to avert mental suffering, before it gets a chance to take hold of us? All, of course, without needing a car to be careening out of control toward our physical bodies! Can we consciously suspend a typical reaction, before we become entirely submerged in it, long enough to provide a different way to react and respond? We would not necessarily completely delete the reaction, but such an act would certainly take the teeth out of such an extreme response significantly. It would enable us to be calmer, more reasonable, and less controlled by the reaction. For this to happen, we must *really want* to free ourselves from mental suffering. If we enjoy our suffering, the way many people actually do, then we won't seek to be free of it. We need to ask ourselves whether we enjoy our own suffering, whether we need it to feel alive or whether we want to feel alive but in a far richer and fuller way, which is what *this* is about. I understand how using the term "enjoy suffering" sounds absurd but notice how we often want to hold on to the suffering over something; there is a need to wallow, commiserate, and whine. We often get angry at people who try to take us out of our own bad mood, almost as if we want or possibly enjoy the suffering we are attached too. This is one of those truths about humanity that astounds us because it is counter-intuitive to what we might think but if you openly and objectively observe your-self you will realize that it is true—many of us are terrified of what life would be like without the drama of the suffering we feel we "deserve". In other words—"don't take the suffering away from me or else I will feel existentially naked and exposed to the world"!

The gist of this concept is to elevate our conscious awareness to a new speed of processing. By "not thinking about it" or "not remembering it," we deprive our mind of brooding uselessly, as it almost always tends to do. By virtue of self-observation, we become increasingly aware of ourselves so that the anticipation of our own reactions are clear and distinct. I want to quickly add that the person may not be ready to let go of that suffering, which adds to the complexity. What I am speaking of requires a "readiness", if the person is not ready to let go, he or she will be helplessly defensive. To make this idea of developing an aversion to our often deceived minds (innocent as they are), or a mind that is engaged in utter non-sense, consider another quick example taken from everyday life, and let's follow it together:

> *You are eagerly waiting for a response in the form of an email relative to whether or not you are hired at a job you need desperately. Tension and anticipation is building as you anxiously and impatiently keep peering at your phone for the email. After twenty or thirty minutes, you see a portion of the message on your phone that reads: "We are sorry to …" These words cause immediate fear, anger, and rejection as you shudder*

in disappointment and desperation. You don't even read the entire message, and within that split second, you walk away from the phone, unable to bear the words of rejection in order to give yourself time to collect your composure as you mull what this means to your future. Your body is now filled with tension, emotionally you feel hurt, and your mind is frantically imagining different alternatives now that you are still without a job.

Before we go specifically into neuralizing, consider that these reactions are common and go on all the time. Of course, they are all not as serious as this one, but we are almost always reacting, jumping to conclusions, and creating misery for ourselves in the privacy of our minds relative to just about everything that happens. Whereas most people can relate to this example, and while it is true that some people would grab the phone, open the email, and embrace the apparent bad news by fully reading the email and what it says, that is not what is important for our purposes. What is critical is that one who practices self-observation would have been conscious of the rush of the reaction that occurred in that instant and not become *fully* embroiled in the response. They would experience a sense of themselves apart from the reaction, almost as if it were someone else's reaction—kind of like you were watching this person in a movie, *yet it is you.* This is the extraordinary idea of having what some teachers refer to as creating inner space or a moment of objectivity before you are engulfed in your mini nervous breakdown. It is in this instantaneous, high-speed, rarely perceived split second that neuralizing can occur. To "not think it" would mean that your consciousness intuitively, in the form of a premonition, and due mostly to self-observation, brilliantly diverts the attention away and intentionally veers into a different direction, similar to the first example of dodging the out-of-control car. This deeper level of consciousness knows, without question, all the mechanical reactions to expect if you identify with your usual conditioned response. It is so intent on creating a new inner experience that such a person would rather react differently than back to the same conditioned patterns (their karma). This is all happening at light speed of course, which is why it is of higher consciousness and requires a higher amplitude of energy.

The key reason *why* a person seeks higher awareness or higher consciousness as opposed to remaining in his or her old self lies in what typically might happen next in this same example involving the email. Consider that after that same person saw the first few words of the email, after brooding and delving into self-hate about his lost job opportunity, he opens the email—now that he has sufficiently paid the price by suffering—and reads the entire message: "*We are sorry to* have taken so long to inform you but—congratulations! You have been accepted into this position in our company."

If we share the same urge to evolve past our current state of consciousness, then this example might cause a chuckle, but it should make us mad as well. If our own consciousness is not bothered by how the mind is so easily duped and how we spend so much time lost in the smoke and mirrors of assumptions, incomplete information, and our own outlandish concoctions of what is going on, then there is no hope we will seek to change. Neuralizing is an advanced strategy of curtailing many of our own reactions before they can fully form because, as an experienced student of self-observation, we realize that by the time we become aware that we are upset, it is too late. Once we are steeped in an emotional reaction, it is, as mentioned earlier, like having the flu and wishing you had taken your flu shot. Just like we cannot wish away a bad cold or can't simply smile and ignore depression or anxiety, we are lost in the clutches of this emotional state. We can, however, limit their ability to start by engaging mental practices to diffuse the states that contribute to this unusual adventure. To flesh out this idea of neuralizing in one other way, Jan once described it as hearing a faint echo of an internal reaction before it manifests. In other words, before it becomes a full-blown physical, emotional, and intellectual experience. As an analogy of this practice, he referenced the phenomena in certain musical recordings where a faint echo of the first few notes is heard a split second before the actual record starts playing (this is evidenced in the original recording of Led Zeppelin's song "Heartbreaker" on *Led Zeppelin II*). Imagine hearing a pre-echo of your pending inner emotional reaction to ordinary life experiences. It is in this subtle and elusive moment that neuralizing can occur. You hear the echo of a pending reaction and shake your head or shift your eyes suddenly away before you are fully immersed in the reaction. Or, to have some fun with this, imagine delivering bad news to a person who can't stop dancing while they hear bad news. The dancing body makes it almost impossible for the mind to lament and grieve. Applying this practice usually requires high levels of attention, a storehouse of observations, and a deep longing to alter one's state of consciousness and being. Neuralize the meaning of this concept and don't sweat not getting it. Just move on and come back to it if you are drawn to it. I will refer back to this idea in some of the pages to come to provide more examples, but for now, let's continue to the third mental practice of changing the way we can process information.

3. Assimilation of New Consciousness and the Energy of Kundalini

My personal experience actively combined all of the above as I have sought to assimilate everything I learned about higher consciousness and apply it to what I found beneficial and transformational. What was unique for me was the way I absorbed the radical Kundalini experiences and worked daily to merge them into one coherent whole. My attention would dart from strange manifestations in the body to incongruences I would observe in emotion, while simultaneously having flash visions of multiple observations and memories in my mind. Strangely, this was never overwhelming to me because everything happened at a pace that my being had calibrated over time. In retrospect, it was the accompaniment of having what I referred to earlier as a *transcendental aim* that provided me with guidance that tempered the integration of these various experiences. I want to make it clear, however, that I was in a constant battle with the typical neuroses that we all struggle with, and by no means was I free of fear, hostility, and sadness. As mentioned several times, emotions are fast and powerful and take full hold in an instant. This inner work is not easy, and like the bodybuilder, it takes work over time (unless, again, the aspirant is unusual or born to enlightenment). The key point is that in order to evolve a new way of processing information, we need to pay attention to how we process change and how we respond to challenges. As human beings, we need to be trained on how to live as whole integrated beings instead of living fragmented and therefore conflicting mental lives. The old maxim, a house divided against itself can't stand, communicates deep truth. The aim must be to establish a footing on firm ground to see the whole so we can work on the disparate parts. A higher perspective is needed for this, as is a longing to be unified within. A higher, faster, and more efficient intellect doesn't spin unnecessarily in senseless worry, unresolved anger, and depressing mental scenarios (although they will continually appear as if you never worked on your-self for a single moment). We need to relax the tension in our body, short-circuit the conditioned patterns of negative emotion, and use higher processes of the mind to blaze new pathways of perceiving and living life. The following two revelations helped me to understand the mystical levels of consciousness and how they reflect in human life. They are personal to me but delivered rare and wonderful insights that propelled this journey forward.

• Teachers and the Mystery of Improvisational Wisdom

I remember sitting on a dock observing life and nature, reflective and comforted by the profound intelligence that surrounded me, when a bird landed a few feet in front of me and began to sing. Within a few seconds, another bird came from a distance, landed next to her, passed a small fish from his beak to hers that he had just caught, and flew off. Clearly, there was a flow of communication within the realm of the birds that was synchronized, organized, and part of their collective intelligence. One bird catches the food for the other, and this is communicated through birdsong. I was intrigued and kept looking at the bird, wondering how *the song* formed. Where did this song actually come from? How did it start? Why that particular song? And even more profoundly, how did the birds come to agree on the meaning of the songs in order to ensure their survival? We know they did not discuss it, debate, vote, or write it into law. Nature does this, and millions and trillions of other things just like it, without the format of intelligence that humanity uses to achieve progress and technology. There is a silent flow of prodigious and ancient intelligence right before our eyes in every second that transpires. We visited this idea earlier relative to flight, spider webs, and butterflies. In this particular observation of birds that sing, my consciousness couldn't help connecting this wondrous part of nature to the way communications flow through humanity. Humanity uses thousands of different languages and forms of communication, and similar to the bird, there is no prescript. Words fly out of our mouths replete with

114

order, diction, punctuation, feeling, and, most importantly, a high grade of information without us really thinking about it. It simply happens—and usually so fast we barely remember what we say. It does get more complex than this, but the point is that a much higher level of intelligence (and not a white-bearded man in the sky) is behind every conceivable nuance of life's intelligence. When it comes specifically to teachers of higher consciousness and spirituality, it is perplexing how such voluminous wisdom flows through them, resulting in thousands of hours of extemporaneous and spontaneous talks. Teachers like Jan Cox, Krishnamurti, and most recently, Eckhart Tolle, among many others, speak for decades without a teleprompter. This certainly is not unique to spiritual teachers, but the mystery of the flow of coherent intelligence from an unknown source should not go unnoticed. In the context of Kundalini, there is also a narrative that derives its source from that same unknown mystery, but it is the sophistication of this flow that is striking. Earlier, I referenced how the collective intelligence of more than four billion years of evolution lives, moves, and communicates, and it is part of our purpose to channel and align this intelligence so it can communicate with optimal precision.

Gopi Krishna, who I referenced earlier as one of the most influential teachers of advanced Kundalini, delivered writings and talks that surpassed anything ever heard before relative to this subject matter. This is the essence of the mystery: *how do human beings, whether they are of scientific, musical, or spiritual origin, create and deliver such elaborately textured communications and creations without piecing each theory, note, or idea together, one building block at a time?* When any of us discuss, or better yet, argue about a topic, doesn't this all happen far too fast for us to weigh, contemplate, and analyze every nuance of communication before we speak it? We obviously don't stop to weigh our part in the conversation, yet it all flows with innate and extraordinary fluency. I specifically wanted to make this point because if our attention is not honed in on the miraculous spontaneity of intelligence, then we can miss the true source of creation, and this is essentially important when opening up to higher consciousness. As can be surmised from the detail of the physical experiences of Kundalini, the spontaneity and explorative nature of biological physical life is happening, and our collective consciousness (including yours) is linking to that dimension of evolution. Thus the physical evolution and the conscious intellectual evolution occur in tandem, together, and in unison.

It is an absorbing and fascinating experience to ponder how these insights pour out of these teachers like birdsong and deliver discourses that impact millions of people over long periods of time. As I have touched on a little so far and will develop further later, it is a blissful wonder to sit in silence and leaf through pages of human wisdom. Whether the words are from Buddha, Jesus, and Mohammed, or Dante, Shakespeare, and Wordsworth, the sheer expression and message in such eloquence is reminiscent of nature's wonder. Humanity's songs are much different from the little bird on the post, but consider these words from Wordsworth's poem, "I Wandered Lonely as a Cloud," and think about it flowing out of a very highly evolved, exotic bird (humanity) and how it interconnects with nature almost as if nature herself is speaking through him:

> **For oft, when on my couch I lie**
> **In vacant or in pensive mood,**
> **They flash upon that inward eye**
> **Which is the bliss of solitude;**
> **And then my heart with pleasure fills,**
> **And dances with the daffodils.**

Wordsworth's "inward eye" and the "bliss" that emanate from "solitude" is the very realm I am referencing and the place from which a higher consciousness derives the improvisational wisdom I am speaking of. As mentioned in the section prior, the magnificent flow of creative wisdom does not just flow freely through spiritual teachers but from virtually all human creativity, whether it be poetry, music, art, movies, theater, and so on. The point I am making is that our own very conscious attention needs *to feel the presence* of this astounding intelligence as it flows through our every word, action, and thought. *We are that very intelligence in action right now.*

• Higher Consciousness Aligns with Life's Long-Term Good

As the energy and passion for life hyper-charged my mind, I couldn't help immersing myself in the mystery of how a good part of humanity is driven by a relentless passion to serve the long-term good of life. If we step back from the history of humanity, we see an incredibly inspiring power, an almost invisible force, that lifts our consciousness out of time to ensure a promising and enduring future. As higher consciousness awakens, whether temporarily in, say, a hero who risks his or her life to save another, or in a person who finds their purpose in caring for the sick or feeding the poor, there is an intangible lifting of our spirit to help life thrive and survive. Perhaps the most celebrated trait of humanity, the one that moves and inspire our souls most, is when a person sacrifices herself for the good of the whole at the expense of her own self. Stories of true altruism soar above most other stories and reflect optimal human character. This is essentially important to observe and ponder because it is a considerably uplifting realization and the palpable reality that is evidenced throughout history. Who among us is not rendered silent and respectful of any action that is truly selfless and magnanimous? The higher intelligence of our consciousness recognizes a more evolved aspect in ourselves when we encounter it in our daily and worldly experience. Similarly, when a person helps another, we are moved in a way that is deeper than our ordinary repertoire of emotions. We are uplifted; we are filled with joy and filled with a sense of meaning and hope. We can also notice that often, when psychologically healthy people are confronted with mortality, they find meaning in leaving a legacy of some form—lasting goodness. It often is one of the few things that actually console one who is terminally ill—to do something, leave something, or contribute something that extends past their own limited time. While later in this book I reference very specific experiences that reflect this idea, there is one very moving and appropriate personal experience I would like to pass on now that is relevant to this truth. Without going into all the details, my sister-in-law, Gail Inzerillo, was diagnosed with a terminal condition. Being a wonderful human being who would stop and carry injured animals to hospitals, volunteer her services selflessly, and always be jovial and willing to help people, she felt a deep need to buy everyone she loved a gift. To me she gave a small stone that reads: "Follow your Dreams" which I placed on a table in my room. After she passed several months later, the words on the stone would energize and encourage me to finish this book and pass her positive energy to my reader (you). This is a high level of expression that opens a dimension close to our sense of immortality. This can also be realized in the memories of a life that impacted others in a good and positive way. Our consciousness relishes the good that it has done on the earth and lets go into peace and awe-filled silence. This is one of the most transformative and fulfilling experiences a human being can have because, at this point, the diatribe of negative emotion and paranoid thought have lost their hypnotic hold; one surrenders to the ultimate inevitability because the highest levels of energy are free to flow and emanate without conflict and tension.

The effort to elevate one's consciousness in a single lifetime is a commitment to the long-term good of life, an unspoken and deeply felt drive that warrants no explanation. The most advanced spiritual masters and teachers appear to operate without any sense of time. They act from such a high level of being that it is almost beneath them to talk about it or corrupt it with words. An extraordinarily coherent system of teachings flows through them for the entirety of their life, as if the teachings are sacred and so much larger than they are. As much I personally found such exciting wonder in the intelligence that manifests in nature, it all pales in comparison to stepping back and looking at the teachings of a Lao Tzu, Buddha, or Jesus. They clearly operated from a different plain than ordinary people. It is stupefying to think that their teachings and lives are impacting the very words I am writing thousands of years after their passing, and those who are reading these words are therefore processing the energy they delivered in those few short years that they expounded their teachings. It is equally astounding that no matter what degree of evil befalls humanity, the wisdom of the long-term good overwhelmingly presides. Just take a walk around the Freedom Tower in NYC today and silently peer, think, ponder, and behold. Life's indomitable spirit is unquestionable and leaves no doubt as to whether it has unshakable integrity. Evil is no match for the good over the long term, no matter how much it hurts in the moment. If you think life is catastrophic, evil, and ultimately negative, ask yourself, mathematically, how many times you've been up against a wall with a gun to your head in a state of abject terror. Most of us today spend our days with lattes, being entertained by our phones, and are almost never in *real* danger. It is mostly the idiotic stream of words that flow in our brains that cause the havoc we encounter. This does not discount the days when there *is* challenge and illness. Those moments are real, but we should do the math for the sake of peace of mind. We live our lives safely over 99 percent of the time. We go to bed at night quite comfortably as we finally roll our heads into a soft pillow, close the lights, and drift off into warm bliss as the gibberish mind finally recedes like a faint narrative that is babbling on about unvalidated nonsense. We then vanish into temporary oblivion (if you are one of the many people today who can't or don't get enough healthy sleep due to incessant worry, please try and give your-self this 6-8 hour break before returning to the agony the next morning if you so choose - you deserve a break and life is short - also, you can be sure it will still be there waiting for you to wake-up the next morning). Again, the point I am making is that we are better off if we focus our energy on gratitude and respect for the long-term good in life and use it to motivate and press on toward our most valued personal goals. The challenge is to apply an active mind and not get lost in the temptations of negativity. Negativity is easy, negativity is lazy, and negativity is profitless.

• Awakening and Enlightenment

This last segment closes out the intellectual dimension of my Kundalini experience. To review where we are, I enumerated fifteen manifestations of the body, explored how emotions were elevated and found new evolution through a variety of mediums and entertainment, and now in this section, I am detailing how my intellect found new frontiers of expansion through divergent ways of processing information and applying wider perspectives to the activities of everyday life. Before delving into the final wrap-up and how this all comes together, I want to address my understanding of what is usually referred to as conscious awakening and enlightenment.

Over the years, I often found myself asking, what exactly am I looking and striving for in this engagement with esoteric conscious evolution and Kundalini energy? How do they fit together? Are they connected? Am I confident there is a purpose to all this or could it all be an extraordinary and outlandish aberration or error? Can it be a bizarre abnormality that I have spun into an elaborate story? These questions are partly frightening to me but mostly exhilarating. There can be no doubt that this experience has been fiercely alive, has manifested with unshakable determination, and now, through this very writing, is seeking full expression. As I write these words in the spring of 2018, only a handful of people know I am writing a book, and those people couldn't be more perplexed by what I could possibly write a book about (other than salesmanship perhaps). As mentioned in the first chapter, my aim was to explore the highest grade of human experience with the hope of understanding what life is from *that* vantage point. At the time, I had no idea what I was in for and how it would play out over the next four decades. The ideas of awakening and enlightenment would appear frequently in many of the systems I studied as I struggled to understand what exactly those concepts actually meant and more importantly, are human beings capable of living such a life. At what point does one start *"awakening"*, and how would we differentiate that state from simply being spiritual or mentally healthy and happy? Is enlightenment an assured state of being that results from work on oneself, or is it an elusive dream that captures our attention but never quite delivers that momentous moment of exultation and total freedom? The questions are endless, but I have come to realize that *in the world of words, concepts, and ideas, there is no such thing as awakening and enlightenment.* They are words that reference a distinct process that we can agree on, but they are not real the way a table or a chair is real. Thus, we are left with words that we should never adamantly defend and, most importantly, never claim we have achieved. Enlightenment and awakening can be looked upon as a process that some people are engaged in (most are not), that is extremely subjective and largely obscure. To this point, I always remember the ending of the *Wizard of Oz* where the Scarecrow, the Tin Man, and the Cowardly Lion were awarded brains, a heart, and courage in the physical form of a diploma, a testimonial, and a medal of courage, because such intangible things like intelligence, feelings, and courage *do not have* a measurable form. They needed to be represented as animate objects even though it was *the experience* that was the reward. Awakening and enlightenment are words; the experience is something only we can know for ourselves, *without the words.* The experience is a wonderful journey that defies definition. In this vein, I also often remember the lyrics of Jimi Hendrix in the song "Are You Experienced" where he sings from an almost supernatural realm the words, "Are you experienced? ... Not necessarily stoned but ... beautiful." The word "beautiful" in this context can mean a blissful natural place of being without the fetters of judgments, competition, definitions, measurements, anxiety, and exasperation. To *be*, to *breathe* and *just live*—not to run away and escape like a frightened child. This is because we have observed, watched, applied consciousness, and now know it simply makes sense not to disappear completely in self admonishment but do everything we can to break free and live. No matter what trauma, grief, misfortune, or catastrophe befalls us, those of us who are living above ground must live well, live strong, and live with determination and patience. The alternative is hell.

Traditionally, awakening and enlightenment are best explained as the process of consciousness becoming conscious of *itself.* The more consciousness bathes in itself, the less it can remain identified fully with the body, emotions, and mind. Conscious awakening has often been compared to awakening from sleep in bed; we awaken out of a dream and find ourselves comfortably rolled up in blankets with our head resting on a pillow. The nightmares and dreams are now a faint memory that lingers for a second or two; that is usually the extent of pain from a nightmare. For one seeking to awaken and engage the process of enlightenment, the aim is to experience thoughts almost as dreams. The dreams become like bubbles you pop with the needle of self-awareness, and they literally vanish—just like bubbles do. In Zen, we often hear of how the Zen master asks a pupil an impossible question (known as a Zen Koan) that has no rational answer. As the pupil becomes lost in the mental narrative dream of trying to answer the question, the Zen master smacks him on the head with a stick to instantly break the trance of solving the problem (the process of "problem solving" vanishes). The pupil suddenly has no problem to solve. He only feels the sting of the stick while he looks at the smiling face of his Zen master— simply aware in the present moment without a single thought, awake and enlightened (at least for that moment). This is also why it is ironic that a true movement toward enlightenment is more about *seeing* and less about possessing traditional knowledge.

My experience of awakening and enlightenment is that the more I struggled with the concepts, the more entangled I became in results, and the more anxiously I demanded change, the more I lost the very essence of the enjoyment of the journey. The real energy was in the exploration and inner adventure. Many times when I would start measuring my progress, I would feel an invisible Zen master swipe me with a stick. The process is using everything in our personal lives, especially adversity, to remember to break the automatic mental narrative and frolic in the fun by basking in the outlandish genius of life by finding new ways to enjoy liberation. Everything from hysterical laughter, to the rapturous joy of a peak experience, to exploring messages and teachings in movies, plays, poetry, and books, to sitting silently in nature and watching a spider weave her web should all be part of the joyful romp through the absurdity of existence. If we do not choose this path, we are left to suffer, stew in self-pity, and fret in mental concoctions we ourselves create (this is the hell I referenced earlier). Not a wonderful option. Which option do you prefer? But before you answer, remember that the option toward freedom takes work (if you choose to call it that; I rather call it *play*). The true ultimate present that life bestows on us all is that our awakening lies in our own thread of personal life that only *we* can live and find out how it all connects to deliver *our very own* enlightenment. I understand that such a message generates many questions because it feels impossible to *not* take thoughts seriously like *I lost my job, my loved one is sick*, or *I have a terminal disease*, but if we don't creatively move our consciousness from that repetitive narrative, we are again doomed. We need to *feel it*, scream and cry when necessary, throw something against the wall (without hurting anyone), and then take the high road up and out. *That* is higher consciousness, *that* is awakening, and *that* is a form of enlightenment. We ought never to stew in guilt or embarrassment for too long. We naturally are what we are but are better off with a light on in our heads that seeks to forge forward and grow. When higher intelligence becomes active it seeks to separate from that which we call "I", the "me" of the lives we have lived up to that point – again it does not completely vanish (we can hear our old selves mumbling and grumbling), but in our highest moments it is suddenly as if we are starkly alive and completely fulfilled - no past, no future, no thoughts, no escapes, no questions, no worries, and most importantly – no sense of time because the "you" or "I" that registers time and suffers over time no longer exists to needle and disturb us. We are free of all the maniacal idiocy our irrational egos and lower emotions subject us too– we wake up without the torment of being who and what *we were*. In a sense, and I mean this strictly internally, it is like we suddenly stop showing up for that same game we have been losing every day of our lives and the experience of such a state is breathtakingly peaceful—*Ahhhhhhh!!! . . . And no one in the outside world, would or could, notice we stopped showing up (again, this is all an internal private party).*

SECTION IV

Wrapping up Spiderwebs, Physiology, and Consciousness

I will now tie together many of the ideas, experiences, and speculations that we have explored and link them together in a discussion of the transformation that we can make possible in our sojourn through life. As I have alluded to already, there is a central thread that is weaved through these writings that I hope touches us in a similar manner. That thread has nothing to do with the personal details of either my life or yours. It has to do with striking that match of wonder that encourages a creative contribution from every one of us no matter our time, place, or position in life. There is only one place to start from, and that is the very moment we are all in—*right now*. From a higher perspective, there is no past and there is no future, as evidenced by the fact that our minds have to recall a past moment or project a future time and place. Before delving deeper into where all this might lead, it may be helpful to articulate the basic perspective that has been my driving force. What I mean by perspective is the larger picture, kind of like the complete image of a jigsaw puzzle before the attempt to piece together the individual pieces, the blueprint that drives the total mass of our lives. As we all proceed in this extraordinary journey, it is healthy to ask ourselves *if we even have* a perspective that pulls together the pieces of our individual life. It is quite a challenge and very much like searching amid smoke and mirrors, because our progress seems to appear and disappear by the moment. It can, though, reap enormous transformative benefits.

The perspective from which I have written starts with the big picture of life itself. We need to encompass the fact that life is transpiring from a vast evolution that, as evidenced by our history, we need to be very careful about relative to our own consciousness. We see on a daily basis how cruel, unconscious, un-empathic, and selfish we can be and the results that karma delivers to our lineage. The question for us as individuals is whether we choose to stay on an automatic path and react to life as it unfolds, or do we hold our own ground, dig into our own bunker, look at life with our own consciousness, and lift ourselves into a different orbit. It is clear that this is not at all necessary for the masses but only for those few who are really moved by their own spiritual aspiration to venture out. These few people vary considerably in how they find their own path, create their own journey, and author their own evolution, because no two lives are the same. *It is all individualistic.* We own our destiny if we so choose. For me, my intelligence was restless and questioned the big picture of life before honing in on what became my path. The hope is that by evidencing my own perspective, it will help encourage the energy of my readers in any way *they* find fit. I am fully aware that much of what I have written may not have touched the reader and may even have caused resistance, criticism, and rejection. All that is expected, but if you have found this story intriguing, let's continue together on a review of the perspective and how it all comes to fit into one tapestry. The following will first outline the detail of a higher intellectual perspective before I return to the more practical applications in our daily lives and specifically my dual life and how all this crystallized into my life as a salesman, a family man, and one just like all of us who are finding our way through the wonder of life.

The Larger Perspective of Life

The big picture of life has been the governing inspiration for my personal view. As we have seen, life, although profoundly mysterious, is growing explosively through intelligence and creativity that is observable and literal. I feel the need to reiterate the fact that I am speaking more from biology, action, and physical reality than a conceptual philosophy. Life itself is perfectly capable of rendering things we would normally label as miraculous, although we don't tend to experience them that way. Higher orders of intelligence are alive and operational *in us* as they are in nature and actively seeking their next incarnation through our thoughts, actions, and visions. I pointed out just how uncanny the physical manifestations of life are in that life, through nature, can produce just about any substance and accomplish just about any feat of extraordinariness in order to survive, thrive, and grow. I invite and implore all of us to look openly and objectively at nature, from her fantastic designs, to her imaginative creative solutions, to her sheer and expansive diversity. Each of us ought to consider seeing the world as a child does with limited filters and comments but also with penetrating curiosity. From this perspective, we can revisit the idea that life most certainly can and will continue its course of evolution *through* humanity by introducing new physical energies, higher emotional experiences, and a next generation of mind and consciousness in which we can process life anew. Today, we have far more excitement, hope, and anticipation for the next iPhone or cutting-edge app than we do for the next stage of human conscious evolution and the new features it may deliver to our personal lives.

By intentionally seeking to create and encourage the production of higher energies, it becomes possible to envision some of the potential experiences I have spoken of. My search has been an exploration of what human experience can evolve into. I realized that a philosophy of life would not be enough to answer the existential question I raised as a teenager, but an exploration into the experience of life and humanity could be fulfilling and exciting—which it has been. It is beneficial and enjoyable to remind ourselves of all the supremely positive experiences that create energy—from the ecstatic physical energies of laughter, sex, and endorphin highs of the body, to the emotions of love, caring, and gratitude, to the intellectual heights of learning, creating, and exploring. The next question is whether life can take these enriching and empowering experiences to another level, one that might account for Kundalini activation, deeper connections and relationships with life itself, and a consciousness that processes life on multiple dimensions simultaneously, where there is less suffering and more optimism and growth.

The experiences I have outlined hopefully suggest a possible vision of human experience as wide and extraordinary, with potential that we are just beginning to tap into. Kundalini energy can very well be life's way of introducing a higher octane and higher voltage of physical energy into the body that is needed for a new expansion. Kundalini experiences are, again, not new; they have been documented in different ways and under different guises for thousands of years and were most notably documented (for me) by Gopi Krishna, as previously mentioned. It is important not to get sidetracked by the word *Kundalini* in that it represents the bio-evolutionary energy that is at the basis of all creation but can possibly manifest in a variety of ways without any restrictions and rules. All experiences that feel good and that catalyze excitement, fascination, and joy are manifestations of this energy and need to be consciously nurtured and explored. We all need to *feel* the energy of creation flowing through us as it occurs in order to get a sense of what I mean. One of the main reasons I included the observations of nature and how she creates new substances (like the silk of a spider) and the boundless capabilities of life to forge new ground (like flight), is that it *is biological proof* that new creative manifestations are beckoning and evolving before our eyes, if we look over broad periods of time.

Kundalini energy experiences can be an emerging dimension of human evolution that accesses the masterful blueprints of nature to introduce the next level of human consciousness. We need to consider that this is not only possible but, more or less, a continuation of exactly what life has been doing for more than four billion years. An enticing question to ponder for oneself is, Why would it stop with us? Why would this grand creation cease, as opposed to continue to manufacture newly fascinating creations? And do we recognize that those creations are now in the form of music, literature, and psychological transformation, as opposed to a third arm, a second head, or physical wings to fly? (*Our* flight includes helicopters, jets, and rockets, which carries evolution into new vistas and frontiers). All human technology is evolution – technology *is* our wings to fly (just not with feathers). The new music that is flowing through portals of the internet, ITunes, and on stage through improvisation, *is* our new evolution - literally and viscerally not theoretically.

Another notable meditation to ponder is how that same overwhelming genius and power of creation is now working on *our* conscious evolution. We have very good reason to be hopeful because life is quite good at surmounting odds, being creative, and persisting over eons of time. It is only our little minds and childish egos that imprison us in stagnant, dark, and pessimistic mental states. I would also urge those who feel this rising sense of wonder and yearning to explore higher consciousness to research any of the teachings and teachers I have explored (and some you may uncover yourself). Without question, seek out other teachers that appeal to *you*. Spiritual teachers vary and are not for everyone. It's true that as our consciousness rises, we can understand all true teachers of higher consciousness, but certainly, in the beginning, we can become captivated by those who appeal to us personally. The best teacher of all, of course, is life itself, but as it is written in the Gospels, it is for those who have ears to hear and eyes to see. If we remain angry, hostile, bitter, and selfish (in a non-productive way), we have no chance of change and transformation. Also, regarding this idea, we don't want to be duped into thinking negatively about life because of war, famine, disease, and suffering. Although we are all horrified by these realities, we must see that these are inevitable necessities for the growth of life and to run away from them and escape leads to psychological trauma. Every living flower must eventually wilt and die before our eyes, and *we* are not privileged exceptions. Remember to look at life not as still-frame photography but as a film moving into the uncharted future – we really have no choice but to peer in awe and embrace what *is* and how it is all evolving.

Back to a More Personal View and Where It Leads

As I experienced the various manifestations of electricity that manifested as sensations, powerful jolts of sudden and abrupt shocks, the feeling of an unfamiliar energy in my limbs, face, and torso, and all the other physical phenomena I have described, I was continually taunted by whether the whole syndrome could be explained as a malady of my nervous system. As the entirety of this experience unfolded, I had to act as if nothing was happening, mainly because I myself did not know what was going on. I already knew how frivolous it was to talk about such odd topics with people who had no interest. Again, I was never around people who shared these interests in any way or any form. I literally became like Batman, who had two entirely different identities—although my secret one was certainly no hero to anyone. My mind was always highly active with insights and efforts to understand my inner world, but it knew instinctively how to camouflage itself when I would make a sales call, help with the kids, or be out with people for dinner and holidays. My attention would be alertly recording observations while I fully enjoyed the social interactions and everyday encounters. Thankfully, these ordinary worldly experiences were in such contrast to the internal experience that they served as a continual reminder to try to piece it all together and added more useful friction for my internal life. *They all fueled the inner search.* The fascinating truth is that it all connected flawlessly into one comprehensive unity that catalyzed the expansion of consciousness. For me, everything was always *connecting*; this process of connecting is the entire gist and driver of the experience of conscious evolution. While the unusual new manifestations occurred in my body, and as greater surges of excitement and enjoyment filled my inner life, I observed that the one key to all growth was this one concept of connecting and making connections. Think about the following:

What life and humanity enjoy and value most is making new connections or experiencing new connections.

This seems like an obvious and simple fact but consider the context of our own happiness and well-being. Any connection we make, whether it is physical touch, receiving a smile from a distance, or a conversation with a friend, *alters the cells in our body* even on the subtlest level and causes us to *feel different.* Our lives begin while connected to our mothers through the umbilical cord, which is a direct and essential physical connection. After birth, we need to be held and touched—in other words, be enveloped in connections. Each communication is a connection, and the healthier the connection, the better one feels. On the opposite extreme, consider the barren and forlorn experience of loneliness, a desperate sense of needing to be communicated with, by someone—*anyone!* Feeling abandoned, feeling bored, or experiencing a sense of meaninglessness has a degenerative and draining effect on our life energy. On the contrary, when we start connecting with life, we become energized; every impression from every sense is seeking new and more refined sensations. Touch, sight, sound, smell, and taste all serve to change the chemistry of our bodies literally, (again)not theoretically. Every connection we make contributes to our state of being, and we become increasingly healthy, balanced, and intelligent when we make enlivening and enriching connections. We ought to broaden our understanding of this fact and consider that even the thoughts we allow to play in our heads are *connections*. The way we think is a kind of connection that leads to the connections we have in the world. People connect to themselves, to each other, to their dogs and cats, to their plants, to nature, to music, to movies, to books, and on and on. It is all a living and cascading network of connections. An increase in consciousness means connecting more things together consciously in a comprehensive manner that brings enjoyment and growth simultaneously. In our time in history, life has exponentially expanded connections through texts, Snapchat, Instagram, the internet, Facebook, LinkedIn, and Twitter. Even as I write these pages, my son has been clueing me in on yet another level of connecting through online gaming. This current craze has millions of teenagers and young adults simultaneously interacting and competing on games like Fortnite and Apex, which is exploding into entirely different domains like Twitch, which is speeding up interactions on an ever newer scale. Life's network of interconnectedness has reached a point in which our intelligence, via technology, is reaching into space, instantaneously communicating across the planet, and improving in speed, clarity, and effectiveness at a blinding rate. Just consider how concise a text is. Consider how unnecessary emotion is extracted from these millions of communications taking place every second. Also reflect on the subtle yet astounding effect of *emoticons* as basic emotions are communicated instantaneously with one simple image that sends joy, happiness, love, appreciation, and sadness in a split second. A simple red heart appears on a phone from a person halfway across the world, and energy and cells are uplifted and filled with warmth (this energizing effect on humanity was conveyed precisley in the movie E.T and one of the many reasons it uplifted so many people across the world). Life is energizing itself instantaneously and spontaneously through billions of bits of communication transmitting concurrently throughout its living network. We hardly notice this communication frenzy, and if you watch people's fingers and faces while their bodies enter and respond to these communications, it is downright astonishing, *if not frightening*. Yet, should we be surprised? Remember the caterpillar that flies to Mexico as a butterfly? Should we be surprised, given that the genetic engineering of this living thing we call life has been intercommunicating for billions of years with spine-tingling precision? Conscious evolution in combination with the high-powered physical energy emitted from the human organism can generate exactly this optimal experience that I have been describing all along and what started my search so long ago. We are all transfer and relay stations amid a living, breathing, and expanding creation. *We really should pause and tingle at that fact, we should not be dull and dim-witted to what we actually are (although it is easy to).*

From this vantage point, we can look back at all of the manifestations of higher energy through the body, emotions, and mind that we've explored together and explain them as life forging new connections that lead to a higher interconnectedness of experience. Consider how all this connects to the idea I introduced earlier called neuralizing, authored by Jan Cox. Jan defined this term as the conscious practice of "remembering something without thinking about it." This is an astounding way of processing information. It is mental processing occurring at lightning speed with zero toleration for personal suffering (if you bristle or get unnerved by this statement you are coming from exactly the place we are looking to shatter). A piece of information appears in one's head as a thought or an image, but our mental reaction is digested and repurposed for the long-term good in seconds. We do not allow it to start repeating on us like bad food. Instead, the information is held temporarily in abeyance while our consciousness remains free to move in an alternative direction. In these rare and extraordinary moments, we are given the opportunity to circumvent the hypnotic power of sorrow and suffering. Our consciousness operates at a speed that is too fast for the hackneyed and nauseating repetitive reactions that have tormented us our entire lives. Neuralizing is a new way of processing information that inevitably leads to growth and exploration in place of whining, criticizing, and worrying. This, of course, is very hard to do and does not come easily, but we need to introduce alternative ways of processing this information, or else we stay exactly where we are (ughhh). These ideas are different, but the objective is the same. Ultimately, the objective is to make life a fun romp through time by not only healing ourselves but enjoying the process as we do it. Energy conservation requires a new distribution of energy, a new way of routing energy in oneself so that we can redirect our energy toward growth and conscious evolution. This is the essence of the message—*to forge new intentional connections that relieve suffering and foster a more expansive inner experience of life.* This should feel good, *really good*—and it does. I would add only one additional point, and that is that we all have a genetic constitution that is ours alone to work with. For example, I personally have observed and worked on many neurotic fears and bouts with worry in my own personality. I have also contended with hostility and malice toward people as well as a tendency to get down and saddened by the frequent ugliness of humanity and existence. We all have psychological challenges on multiple fronts. Some are serious enough to be considered a biochemical condition that requires psychotropic drugs, while others have genetic temperaments that border that gray line. It is very challenging to openly face your own temperament without self-judgment, but it is absolutely essential for mental health and well-being. My personal view is that *we are all nuts*, and we should all start from there—and with a really good sense of humor whenever possible. There is absolutely nothing wrong with the use of drugs, and it may very well be necessary for whatever period of time is required until you feel grounded and ready to take on life without the use of drugs (I am talking about prescribed drugs). The key is whether we have developed a state of mind that values the aim to heal and become better than we are now. Again, as referenced earlier, this is *The Work,* and it doesn't come easily. Our consciousness needs to expand enough to encompass the *old us* and the *new us* simultaneously; this can only happen with higher consciousness. It is working with our own attention that we nourish consciously that we can then turn loose on our own existence. We take it seriously, but we also enjoy the ride and always keep our degree of seriousness in check. Being too serious is a mistake—a big mistake (that is why I encourage watching a lot of comedy). On a personal note, I would have to break out of trances of reactions to people and my job by taking a quick walk around the block; or retreating to one place of private refuge we always have—the glorious bathroom! We can be in almost any situation, and if it is communicated properly, we can excuse ourselves, take a breath, smile in the mirror, and return to the situation. It is like a cosmic pass out of every situation. We just can't abuse it, or people become suspicious (why is that guy always going to the bathroom)? Think about this for a moment, think about how we return to ourselves and feel a sense of mental relief (along with physical relief) when in the bathroom.

Before we explore specific examples of how these transformations can be applied to everyday life, I want to point out another profound trend in the collective consciousness that also calls for a celebration. While I'm focused mostly on the inner evolution of an individual, life is growing exponentially on a collective scale. Consider how advances in science and technology are hyper-jettisoning every conceivable field into the realm of the extraordinary on a regular basis. While we spend our time lamenting on the good ole days, we don't realize that a growth explosion is at the tip of our fingertips—and we are participating in it by the moment. Billions of people are exchanging communications effortlessly across the earth, with access to vast amounts of data, video, and images that are emblazoning life's growth. Today, thanks to writers, entrepreneurs, and adventurists like Peter Diamandis, Steven Kotler, Ray Kurzweil, and Michio Kaku, among others, there is a current movement often referred to as "futurists." Although futurists can envision the future either negatively or positively, these writers and thinkers are emphasizing the supreme growth through the impact of the right use of human ingenuity through technology (which is again life's latest marvel). As humanity expands its connections through the internet and social media, ideas are spreading faster and more succinctly than ever before, and the challenges of our future are being addressed by greater numbers of people from all over the world. The mentality that accompanies thinkers like these is that virtually everything is as an intriguing challenge and opportunity and not a problem to bring us down into anxiety and depression. The very word *problem* is a deterrent to growth. These are profound ideas that are delivered in best-selling books, but for my purposes, they represent the cutting edge of life as it grows and expands into an astounding future. *Remember that all this evolution is the same ancient intelligence that is behind all of nature.* It *can't* be of a different source because we are all connected to the same origin. If you are one who is of a more cynical view of human nature and don't share my view that humanity is evolving, I can only urge you to look again. From this perspective, the silk of the spider and human technology are both nature's creation, but life had to create humanity in order to get to technology (she also needed to create a spider to get to the silk).

The future of artificial intelligence, robotics, and synthetic biology are just a few of the profound game changers that will ensure inconceivable change for the good of humanity in comparatively short periods of time. Those who resist this momentum out of fear may be trampled underfoot because life relentlessly charges toward survival and perpetuation. Too many people get caught up in the current stream of "bad news" and end-of-the-world mentality, which is always going to be around us as long as we are growing into another stage of life (which we always will be as long as we are alive). Again, we need to be mindful that we are in our infancy. Our recorded human history is less than ten thousand years out of billions, and this explains a lot when we hear the news that speaks only of disastrous world events, out-of-control politics, and world tragedies. It is important to note that, while I am affirming a positive trajectory for the human race, it doesn't exonerate us from enacting a major catastrophe—like nuclear war—but such blatant horrors can also be circumvented with the right efforts. Again, the topic of our discussion is individual conscious evolution, while virtually everything is feverishly connecting on a much higher plane, *simultaneously*. I have often pondered that the human body is made up of roughly one hundred trillion cells, each independently brilliant and specialized, and all working together to keep *us* alive and healthy (in homeless people and Olympic gold medal winners alike). All must contribute to the good of the whole to protect us as individuals. These cells must deal with constant threats, fight disease, depend on our brains for new technology to help the total being survive, and ultimately foster the future evolution of the species. It's important to note that the cells know nothing about one another even though they are inseparably connected. If the cells of the heart were magically introduced to the cells, say, of the kidney, and thought the way we do, they might declare war on the kidney because of how different these two appear to each other! It would take extraordinary "cell intelligence" to encompass the roles of one hundred trillion cells that are collaboratively integrated into a masterpiece of existence, yet the reality is that they all work quite nicely together. In comparison to the engineering of flight in birds and insects, consider how our consciousness is impeccably calibrated to our bio-physiology to such a flawless degree that we don't even *feel* these one hundred trillion cells firing, splitting, growing, and dying every second. This is a miracle!

Do you *feel the cells of your living body?*

Do you *feel* the energy that animates your body (when not stoned)?

More importantly, *who and what* is it that would *feel* your own aliveness in your own body?

It could get spooky or could be enthralling—it is our decision. I choose—enthralling (who is going to stop me)?

Feel the energy of *not* knowing the answers to the above questions, because if you have answers, they are at best incomplete, if not utterly wrong. The kind of free-spirited liberation we seek lives hand in hand with never knowing anything for sure. If it is not clear by now, I want to be sure I emphasize how important it is that every human being apply a rational questioning intelligence to every part of their life. The barrage of information that is coming at us needs a filter, we need to pause and substantiate the information flooding our brains and creating absurd panic. This sense of rationality is the intelligence of nature itself and we must evolve and use it. Our evolution is depending on applying balanced common sense to just about everything we hear and we ought to seek evidence and concrete data so our minds don't spin in uncontrolled mania. Panic and anxiety attacks pervade if we don't ground ourselves and insist on facts and evidence.

Extraordinary Connections, My Mother's Passing, Reflection and Vision

As you have followed my story, I've gone from a spiritually searching teenager to a spiritually transforming middle-aged person who, at the time of writing this book, is still a New York City salesman but one who has reached a point where the communication to others has become unstoppable. My dual life now has an irrepressible need to merge into a new incarnation that carries the past into a new future like the caterpillar's transformation into a butterfly. The very idea of writing this book appeared as an inspiration from a talk by Eckhart Tolle at the Riverside Church in New York City in 2010. It was outlined in the Rose Room in the New York Library when I had time between sales calls. My love of New York City parallels my reverence for nature in that I see the city as an extension of nature. The ultrahigh-speed cutting-edge growth is like watching Genesis happen all over again, as creativity is flourishing everywhere from the new Freedom Tower, to Broadway, to Central Park. Every coffeehouse, hotel, museum, restaurant, and park is crackling with excited people talking, texting, and traveling to their next destination. It is a kinky mix of spiritual ideas and the thriving materialism of New York City that has helped bring this effort to fruition.

I now want to circle back to the beginning of this journey and share some deeply mysterious and profound ideas and experiences I feel need rendering. I want to talk in a more specific manner about conscious connections. Consciously connecting with intention is about using our intelligence, experiences, and life in a higher way. It is about living deliberately and not on automatic pilot. The aim is to elevate our entire personal journey through time and existence. Of course, virtually no one can do this continually. It happens in fits and starts and hopefully increases as one's life presses and marches forward. It is never a good idea to judge or measure progress—just instantaneously note, see, correct, breathe, and keep moving. In other words, *neuralize* your own growth; don't think about it! Keep active, keep growing, and keep forging forward. Forgetting is a natural part of the process, and we should apply and insist on a zero toleration policy of *no self-hate allowed—ever* (I know it is hard). It is about taking the time to personally ponder, remember, and link experiences together with an intention to expand, grow, and evolve. Although this includes external events, the emphasis is on advanced introspection and uncritical self-observation. While I hope I've personally demonstrated this practice throughout my book, it is far more significant that each one of us individually delves into *ourselves*. Each person's life is as unique as their fingerprint and offers value to the collective journey of life as a whole. The intelligence of life is spinning its own neural web to ensure communication via technology.

Three Transformational Experiences

Three very poignant and powerful conscious connections I've made through my life experiences may help demonstrate the value of connecting in this manner. As you may guess, the most valuable and important conscious connection for me is *the company*, which I spoke of earlier as my direct connection to the masterful and total intelligence of the universe. I will focus on three actual experiences (listed below as A, B, and C) and outline the connections to communicate this point. First, I will share a specific transcendental writing from a special poet that lifted me out of time and space. Next, I will divulge an inspiring story involving the health of our son, Richard, and third, I will share a very personal experience involving grief and the passing of my mother to a glioblastoma. I will not go into enormous detail about these experiences because my purpose is in connecting the precious value these experiences delivered in light of the content of this book. However, it is important *to hear and feel* the experiences, so the message is deeply and fully understood.

A. Transcendental Intelligence: Connecting a Poet to Me, to You

The word *transcendental* has an almost a supernatural effect on us. This magical word pulls us out of ourselves for a few fleeting seconds. To transcend means to move above—a lifting out of oneself and out of time. While plants and animals appear bound to the niche of existence they are born to, humanity engulfs the ability to peer above the mundane hypnotic spell of everyday existence and open to a higher dimension that offers new creative energy, exploration, and jubilation. One of the distinct experiences I had rather early on in my journey involved certain writings that lifted my consciousness up just enough to taste that higher state I longed for. Once elevated to that distinct new level, I felt like a child in a new land with endless frontiers to travel. Before we visit this very special poem by Walt Whitman, consider a few quotations from one of the greatest writers of transcendental intelligence in history, Ralph Waldo Emerson:

> *What lies behind you and what lies in front of you,*
> *pales in comparison to what lies inside of you.*

> *Do not go where the path may lead, go instead*
> *where there is no path and leave a trail.*

> *Adopt the pace of nature: her secret is patience.*

Emerson and Walt Whitman are two geniuses who committed their lives and writing to nature and the wisdom of higher human intelligence.

Walt Whitman communicated his extraordinary relationship with life through his poetry, while Emerson did so largely from essays. But to take all wisdom to an even higher level, I want to highlight an example of conscious communication that is explicative of how our own intelligence is intercommunicating over and above time, which is the hallmark of transcendental intelligence. It's not so much the specific example I'm citing that is truly engrossing but how life's higher intelligence communicates over decades, centuries, and millenniums *to itself—through us.* How its wisdom travels miraculously and effortlessly through our nerves and brains almost without our notice. This example will link the masterful poetry of Walt Whitman, who is speaking from the mid-1800s, to the very moment of our very reading it in the here and now. Notice the level of consciousness of both the poet and us as we experience the poem together. Observe whether you are moved, lifted, or might even get the chills or sense of elation reading and connecting to this short poem. Observe any change in your inner being when you read it and whether you can feel *his presence* in yours as if he is here with us now. If so, it is an astounding connection to behold. Here is a little background to help provide perspective before reading the poem:

Walt Whitman was an American poet who was born in Long Island and grew up in Brooklyn, New York. He was born in 1819 and died in 1892. He wrote a book of poems considered to be a classic by most standards, called *Leaves of Grass.* Walt Whitman celebrated life in his poetry with an almost breathless appreciation for just about everything that was alive. He unleashed a joyful, exuberant, and wonderful appreciation of nature, people, and America and was forced to push language to new limits in order to express what he felt so inspired to publish. His writings were clearly the result of a state of consciousness that was unfettered, full of heart, and, most importantly for my purpose, masterful in the way *he connected* just about everything he could possibly put into words. His consciousness basked in the glee of his understanding of how everything is connected and the miracle it was that he was alive to consciously *connect* through his very existence. The example of his writing that I want to share is one in which his consciousness, so filled with love and determination to connect his poetry to everyone (including us now), lifts completely out of time and accomplishes just that—a direct connection to you and me *in this very moment.* To provide a little background on this short poem, it is called "Full of Life Now." He is forty years old, he references that America (which he calls "the State") is eighty-three years old, and he is calling out to people in future generations to *connect* directly to him. In other words, he wants to be friends with (connect to) people in the future that, in his words, are the "yet unborn." Pay close attention to the way he encompasses his own transitory existence and then speaks directly to us as if he had never died … and he makes us wonder even if death has actually separated us! In essence, he is writing from a higher state of consciousness and transcending time and space:

Full of Life Now

Full of Life now, compact, visible,
I, forty years old the Eighty-third year of the States,
To one a century hence, or any number of centuries
    hence,
To you yet unborn these, seeking you.

When you read these, I, that was visible, am become
    invisible,
Now it is you, compact, visible, reading my poems,
    seeking me,
Fancying how happy you were, if I could be with you,
    and become your comrade;
But it is as if I were with you. Be not too certain but I
    am now with you.

                           —Walt Whitman

The last line of this poem has always startled me. Whitman's consciousness, which is the collective consciousness of life speaking through him, broke the shackles of time and space; he was so thrilled, so electrified, and so deeply *connected* with life that he reached out over centuries to those still yet unborn, *which is us now* as we read this poem. My consciousness connected to his consciousness, which connected to your consciousness as you read it. Thus, the evolution of consciousness is emerging and interconnecting over centuries and millennium. This idea, of course, applies to everything and is why no energy is wasted even though it may appear to be. Everything we say, do, and think is part of an immense interconnectedness and the reason those who have sensitivity to this are drawn to raising our level of consciousness. It's not really us but life itself that is growing and evolving *through us*. Wherever we are and whoever we are at any place in life is significant to the whole. In the analogy of the body mentioned earlier, there are one hundred trillion cells, and all are contributing to the life of the body; not one cell is out of place or not part of the whole. *It can't be.* Higher consciousness works to ignore *all* of the inner voices that childishly dwell in self-pity, erroneously imagining they do not have an important role to play. If you are breathing, you are part of it, and it is a literal, biological reality we are *connecting to*, not an imaginary image in the sky. We are that very fabric of life that has been growing and expanding for billions of years, and now it is our purpose to make conscious connections that interconnect to the next step of that growth and evolution.

B. Life's Collective Evolution Relative to Health and Well-Being

Health, well-being, and conscious evolution are intimately linked for one good reason: good health generates not only a higher *quantity* of energy but a higher *quality* of energy—and conscious evolution and creativity require both. If we recall, I found my way into the study of higher consciousness through the Institute of Self-Development, which although it was a holistic health center that provided treatments in acupuncture, Amma therapy, herbs, and chiropractic services, also had a Western doctor on staff to provide balance. My father was an internist who, at the time, did not accept and welcome the Eastern approach of energy medicine, and we would have debates on its validity and integrity. I was neutral on the subject matter since I was skeptical about energy myself, even though I was immersed in practicing Tai Chi, Chi Kung, and Hatha Yoga, not to mention the Kundalini experiences that unfolded over the years. A part of me was torn trying to reconcile the two sides for quite some time, as I wanted to bridge the two into one total solution of good health. It was only the extremists on both sides who really couldn't see how they could complement each other, but I was always more compelled by a larger and more expansive perspective of the health and well-being question. My focus was on how life was going to trend in the decades and centuries to come, knowing about my own Kundalini experiences and the supreme intelligence of life. As I saw it, Eastern approaches to health were more personable, asked more questions, and treated the entire being physically, emotionally, and mentally, while Western medicine traditionally drove directly at the symptoms with medication. There was also more prevention involved in Eastern approaches and more responsibility placed on the patient to tend to themselves. Western medicine was more effective in urgent care, surgery, and severe diseases, not to mention the invaluable role of the technology of X-rays, MRIs, and CAT scans. Although much of this is changing today on many levels, I wanted to communicate a specific example involving our son, Richard, and his extraordinary success with both Crohn's and Celiac disease using a combination of Western medicine, acupuncture, and medical marijuana. I will connect my son's story to a much larger example of interconnectivity that is even more encouraging as we continue to look at how higher consciousness is about *connecting more things together* to form an emerging and more encompassing level of collective conscious evolution. Again, all this is relevant because we are exploring how life is evolving higher consciousness through individuals and society simultaneously.

At age fourteen, our son, Richard, was noticeably not growing at the same rate as his peers. He had enjoyed a healthy and active childhood playing sports and running around crazy like most young teens, but we were becoming concerned that he was not maturing on par with his friends in terms of height and weight. Nancy and I had attributed it to genetics and were hoping that he was simply a late bloomer, but it got to a point where we had him tested for potential growth hormones. The blood tests came back indicating that he had celiac, an autoimmune disease in which the body reacts to the gluten in wheat and causes damage to the villi in the intestine that extracts nutrients from foods. This would account for his slow growth and maturation as well as the sudden onset of stomach discomfort and irregular bowel movements. We soon followed up with a colonoscopy and endoscopy to scope the area and found that not only did he have celiac, but he also had another inflammatory bowel disease known as Crohn's. In laymen's terms, this condition meant that he could not eat gluten and would have to be treated for very painful flare-ups and cramps that could arise at any time. He had to stop eating all of his favorite foods—pasta, hamburgers, pizza, and cookies, among many others, and find the most effective treatment for these periodic flare-ups. We initially started with the Western route of medical care with a pediatric gastroenterologist as Nancy, in her customary fashion, transformed her kitchen into a gluten-free environment, while I tried to find every option I could to replace his favorite foods and restaurants with gluten-free options. Together we eliminated gluten from our home and diet and did our best to adjust to the current gluten-free products available at the time. This occurred in 2012, and the availability of gluten-free products has changed significantly since then. Luckily for us, Richard's temperament, although upset about these dramatic changes in his diet, valued the idea of growing and maturing and thus resolved to take on both conditions with dedication and commitment. We were fortunate that he stepped up to this challenge with such maturity, especially since he had to deal with the social implications of a young teenager with many friends.

While we adjusted to this new diet, his discomfort seemed to decrease, although the flare-ups from Crohn's did not. It was just about one year after his diagnosis when a new light was to appear in our lives. Nancy was working at a friend's chiropractic and massage therapy office when the chiropractor, Dr. Sue Shulman, decided to give hours to a friend who had become an acupuncturist. Her name is Rebecca Krauss. Rebecca was not only said to be an outstanding acupuncturist but was also sensitive to gluten and did special work with Crohn's. Nancy made an appointment for Richard, and with typical Western medicine bias, I couldn't see Richard taking needles and was skeptical and doubtful of the efficacy of this kind of treatment on a fifteen-year-old boy.

After the first two treatments, I sat down with him and asked him what he thought. Because he was under eighteen years of age, Nancy had to sit with him while Rebecca worked on him, and he said he was not comfortable, didn't understand it, and wanted to stop. Knowing Nancy, I knew that was not about to happen, since she was determined to give acupuncture and alternative healthcare the best shot - given her cautious skepticism to the overall approach of Western medicine. My personal view was that if he was closed off to its potential, it was going to impede any potential the treatments might have to help him, and I wanted to either stop the treatments or encourage him to become more open and optimistic about this approach. Since I had not met Rebecca yet and since I thought he might be more open if he understood it better, I asked Nancy to arrange a sit-down discussion with Rebecca, me, and herself to discuss his feelings and a plan that might help his attitude. The discussion went extremely well, and I was personally very taken by Rebecca and her highly intuitive and advanced level of being. We decided that I would help explain it to Richard and sit beside him during the treatments going forward to help monitor how he felt and whether we thought it was working for him. The treatments became extremely effective. His flare-ups became minimized drastically, he grew and matured fully, and in the meantime, Nancy found an excellent pediatric gastroenterologist who, although he did not participate in the Eastern approaches, he did not discourage or make negative judgments about them. After a few years and much research, we also added medical marijuana to Richard's treatment, which was proving to be effective with inflammation and extreme pain. By seventeen, three years after his diagnosis, due to this overall team approach, his startlingly strong will and attitude, and our ability to mix Eastern, Western, and cutting-edge uses of not only marijuana but Remicade (a drug issued by our gastroenterologist), the condition is currently under control as Richard attends Brockport College in Rochester, New York, where our daughter, Jenna, graduated and who also helped us identify Brockport as being one of the best colleges in terms of being sensitive to food allergies – including Gluten.

There are several points regarding the topic of conscious connections that I wanted to make relative to this story. First, we should take note of how, because of our history with holistic health, we were open to expanded views on how to approach this medical condition. Many people are either biased, judgmental, or simply uneducated or unaware of alternative methods of healing. Many medical professionals adhere to their own approach and exclude other competitive practices that can either harm their own business or call into question their own efficacy. By integrating these three rather different modalities for our son, we were able to address the condition in a far more interconnected fashion that is currently delivering extraordinary results. Secondly, it is important to note *the level of consciousness* of all of the players in this scenario. Our family had been exposed and were open to as many possibilities as we could entertain; we connected to Rebecca, who is operating on a very high energetic frequency herself and who administers an advanced competency in acupuncture and energy work; the medical doctor was not provincial and was open to all possible health modalities; and the level of intelligence surrounding the medical marijuana field is progressive and maturing at an accelerated rate. The most significant aspect of the story is really the totality of how it all worked together as a whole, which is what collective consciousness is all about. It is this evolving inner consciousness that is rising that is allowing more stories like this to become mainstream.

An even bigger idea is how the collective intelligence of life is responding to something as specific as gluten-free foods and the merging of Eastern and Western medicine. Since Richard's diagnosis in 2012, the gluten-free industry, thankfully for us and all those who are either celiac or gluten sensitive, has exploded into a multibillion-dollar industry, with some of the largest food companies from Kellogg's to Ronzoni, and other food companies that focus specifically on gluten-free foods like Schlar and Udi's. The rising consciousness has also reached the restaurant industry (to some degree with a long way to go) in that many restaurants now offer special menus and take seriously the way food is prepared in kitchens by training their personnel and chefs. This demonstrates the extraordinary responsiveness that is becoming more a part of our culture and hopefully will continue to spread to not only all food allergies but a trend to healthier eating overall. This awareness has also recently been spreading to the fast-food industry, where companies like Chick-fil-A, Smashburger, and Shake Shack offer gluten-free rolls that are of the highest quality they can find, while some of the top names in the fast-food industry pay minimal attention and leave their clients to eat their products and their food without the bread. This is all a reflection of levels of consciousness but also reflective of poor business practices. If one person cannot eat a certain food due to an allergy, than the entire family will seek alternative places to eat and dine, which impacts the flow of millions of dollars. There are many examples of this explosive trend toward better health all around us, and one that is dear to me is the emergence of what is called integrative medicine, which combines alternative medicine with conventional medicine. If we recall the first section of this book, I found my way to this path through a holistic health center. In retrospect, that school was way ahead of its time not only because it offered alternative health care and combined it with the physical arts of yoga, karate, and Tai Chi but because it also had a medical doctor on staff. That was in the early 1980s. I distinctly remember being impressed by this fact because it demonstrated an openness and respect for the value of Western medicine and was not radically biased to one side. Again, it reflected higher consciousness by inclusion and intelligence as opposed to prejudice and exclusion. A potential patient would be examined by a team that included both Eastern and Western modalities, and they would agree on integrative treatment if necessary.

Today we are seeing integrative health emerge in some of the largest hospitals in New York as well as, I am sure, other areas in the country. This new level of consciousness is also impacting media and entertainment, as evidenced by a recent movie my brother, Dr. Michael Mollura, PhD, scored (musically) called *Heal*. This movie exemplifies how new and alternative healing modalities are combining with traditional methods to produce effective results in chronic and potentially terminal cases. The movie stresses the importance of how one's mental attitude impacts positive healing energies of the body that help heal us on all levels, which are often lacking in Western medicine. It is the person that matters, not just the symptoms and biochemistry. All these converging movements are the future transformation that is occurring at this very moment in time. The purpose of mentioning this is to point at the correlation of how both individual levels of consciousness and collective levels of consciousness are interconnecting to forge a more positive and promising future. As it turns out, we need to mine and foster the inner resources of the individual to help us align with the body's own miraculous intelligence to heal itself, to provide the best possible health. The larger and more profound perspective is that life is delivering its spectacular intelligence through the entire health and medical field to ensure a better experience for each individual so they can actualize their full potential. While this can still take quite a while, we ought to remember what Emerson said about the secret wisdom of nature—*patience*. The last critical part of this story is the attitude that Richard brought to this challenge. Richard took this challenge on more as an adult than a child. He fostered a positive mental attitude, focused on the long-term results, and effectively altered the course of his life and health while in High School and now College (a very difficult and daunting time in one's life). He has also been identifying and communicating to me how some young rap artists, like Lil Skies (who Richard created an Instagram fan page for), helps his audience by delivering on mental perspectives that can help our youth to battle through the serious life challenges (depression in his case) through music. Evolving an optimistic mental toughness in our youth is critical to the idea of increasing the collective consciousness of humanity—*they are* the future of human consciousness.

C. Timeless Connections and Conscious Evolution

As we move into this last segment of the book, I want to address those moments in our lives where time appears to stop and memories are emblazoned on our consciousness and interconnect them to the higher states we are discussing. These rare and extraordinary memories are often moments when we are shocked so deeply that they alter our brains permanently in ways that most experiences pale in comparison. My first such memory of this sort came when John Lennon was killed in 1980 and later again when I watched the second plane hit the towers in NYC on 9/11. These are tragic and terrifying events most of us share, but I want to take that same mental phenomenon and interconnect ideas of transformation mainly because of how radical they are. For a quick moment, think for yourself how such experiences are so completely brain altering that *time appears to stop.* There is a moment of absolute silence as all the mental chatter of everyday life vanishes and we experience a truly transcendental dimension of consciousness. At the same time, a completely different type of memory is formed that is unlike remembering your password or friend's phone number. While shocking news of such a magnitude burns these memories permanently in our brains, we all have private and personal memories that have a similar effect, which could include everything from a first kiss, to the birth of our child, to the passing of a family member or loved one. The point is to acknowledge that there are different levels of processing, remembering, and experiencing that alter our consciousness. The more intriguing question is whether we can intentionally *use these memories* to elevate our lives or create memories with the intention to become more conscious. In other words, as we work on ourselves, specific memories serve as powerful transformational vehicles that help expand our perspective. We may even want to ask ourselves whether we currently have such moments in our lifetime when we realized something about ourselves that we remember as if it is happening right now. An example of this could be a shocking realization that we are almost always living with anxiety that instantaneously projects preposterous mental possibilities that frighten and unnerve us. If we never realized that before, and then it suddenly strikes, it tends to create a far more distinct memory in our brain than other memories we hold latent about ordinary things. Please keep in mind that I am not talking about having a basic passing knowledge that we live with anxiety; I am talking about a very stark and surrealistic moment where *we see for ourselves* exactly the way anxiety manifests in our nervous system. It is a timeless moment, a snapshot of *us* and what we are, as if we are seeing ourselves on a movie screen. It offers a feeling of liberation, freedom, and promise—an empowering sense of a way out of a self-concocted prison. Over 99 percent of what our neurotic minds create are unvalidated catastrophes that never happened and never will (I remember Jan Cox once teaching that we worry about just about everything except what actually does happen). That should, at the very least, startle us if not cause outrage and revolution against the way we live this short life we are granted. For this brief moment, recall what I wrote earlier about the feeling of caterpillars on our tongue relative to the idea of despising the inner taste and feeling of living with mental narratives in our heads that just never happened or will happen. We should internally revolt against these mental narratives that have zero basis in reality. They do no good while causing enormous harm. These neurotic mental states are our chief enemies, opponents, and toxins.

In these meta-extraordinary moments of timeless memory, we can consider the possibility that our level of consciousness is raised as a result of these significant events into a much higher, more alert, and more aware state. It is also important to notice the way our bodily chemistry is altered during such moments. I personally remember how my entire body and being was changed during 9/11 due to the dramatic influx of fear and how my attention was frantic about more planes hitting New York City in the moments and minutes that followed the attacks. A change in bodily chemistry is another way of looking at higher consciousness, since there are trillions of cells engaged in such a harrowing and unforgettable event. It is in such moments that we become sobered out of our everyday hypnotic state, that cosmic spell that keeps us sane and in line. We can use these moments to become aware of the different levels of consciousness. If we do not differentiate levels of consciousness, then we are bound to one level of consciousness, which is not what we want as seekers. If a small part of our awareness is not disturbed or disquieted by our ordinary state, then there is no energy to press into more encompassing states. Making conscious connections to another dimension of intelligence (which abounds in nature all around us) is ultimately what this book has been about. The following personal account highlights specific higher states I want to share to support this point. I want to clearly articulate a higher state of consciousness based on a real-life experience and demonstrate how I intentionally processed this *out-of-time* memory to counter grief and loss. Again, I want to remind my reader that it is not the details of my particular experience that are important but a spark I seek to light that one uses to seek out a similar self-fulfilling journey that only a person *can deliver to themselves*. My experience unfolded at a time when it was least expected and under extremely adverse conditions, involving my mother, Gina Mollura, in the last days before her passing on January 9, 2013. The extraordinariness of these connections was not the supernatural state that occurred as much as what we do with that inner state to help us evolve individually.

I cannot remember the exact date, but I remember it was on a Sunday in the fall of 2012. It was a typical Sunday, and I had nothing in particular going on when I got a sudden intuition to visit my mother and father—unannounced. At this particular time, everything was absolutely normal; no one was ill (that we knew of), and all of our lives were chugging along just fine. I drove up to the house, and my mother was carrying two or three grocery bags to the front door. I quickly got out of the car to help her and had one of those distinct and strange moments of seeing a person "in time." If you are not familiar with this experience, it is a type of mental processing when you see someone or something with a distinctive higher quality of perception that is a mixture of seeing with objectivity, gratitude, and love—*simultaneously*. It is the experience everyone has when crying at graduation, hearing the news of someone passing, or knowing that what you are experiencing is an ending—an ending of something you love. You feel the experience with the backdrop of passing time, but your awareness is still and very alert.

I remember that she was herself but slightly remote in a way that irked me in a subtle but noticeable way. I did not make an issue of it, as the visit was fine and nothing else happened that afternoon that struck me as strange. It was, however, the beginning of this experience. My mother was a wonderful, loving person who was full of life, joy, love, and a sense of humor that warmed everybody who knew her. She was the heart of our family, and I was very connected to her (as was my 3 brothers and sister). That same week, on Wednesday night, my father observed that she was dropping things with her right hand, and decided to take her for an MRI. The results were sent directly to my brother, Dan, who is a radiologist from John Hopkins University working at the NIH. He called me and said in a very shaky and rattled voice that Mom had a glioblastoma, which he explained is an aggressive cancerous tumor in her brain.

I remember the news racing through my nervous system and altering every cell in my body (reminiscent of my experience on 9/11) while I instantly ran out to my car to drive to the neurologist's office, where my mother and father were supposed to be. I had not spoken to them because everything happened so fast. I got there, and the building was closed. I received word that they may have gone to St. Francis Hospital, where my father was affiliated and my mother had been president of the guild. I drove quickly to the emergency room at St. Francis, where I found a very different mother and father. Everything had changed, and I tried to hold back the tears that were stinging my eyes. My state of consciousness was in a still, extremely aware, and highly focused place that left absolutely no room for me to mentally suffer in the normal way. The mental nonsense that usually occupied my mind had vanished entirely and was replaced by this altered condition. Seeing my mother, and also my father for that matter, in such an innocent state of vulnerability had elevated my nervous system and consciousness, which was now in a totally different place than I was used to.

That was the beginning of an eighteen-month experience, as we were told would be her most likely fate given the type of tumor and its position inside her brain. In the last week of those eighteen months, my mother had become debilitated and mostly incoherent in that she couldn't communicate clearly to us. On the Saturday morning of the week of her passing, Nancy and I went to the house to be with her and my father. It was that morning that my mother suddenly refused to eat. This was two days after the Christmas and New Year's holidays and immediately after my sister Conni and brothers Michael and Dan had left New York to return home to Florida, California, and Maryland, as if my mother knew and somehow timed things for their sake.

The fact that she'd stopped eating was a strong signal that we had to make the difficult call to hospice that immediately sent an ambulance to transfer her to the hospice facility. I was in her room helping her get comfortable as they prepared her for the move when another quite striking moment occurred that transcended time and lifted us both (my mother and me) into an extraordinary timeless state. For a few split seconds, as I was helping her, she became lucid and alive as if there were no tumor, no problem, *no anything*. She did not speak or even try. She looked deeply into my eyes, kissed me three times on the cheek, and made a connection that lifted us out of space and time and the miserable horror we were both fully absorbed in. There was a strange sense of serene resignation to something we both knew we could not change. My consciousness crystalized in that moment, and it was as if a form of invisible magic, far beyond words, moved within us both at the same time. For those few seconds, we were both free of the absurdity that had become our reality.

These connections are the very thing I am referring to when I say that conscious evolution has extraordinary potential, and it is our responsibility to further its growth and expansion into the future. The story about my mother did not end there, but again, keep in mind the idea of connections *and be sure to start thinking about your own.*

My sister Conni had flown in from Florida soon after we told her that we had to transfer Mom to hospice. Things again happened very fast, and before we knew it, Conni, my father, Nancy, and I were numb as we tried to adjust to what was happening. My mother's condition progressed very fast, and after her two brothers (my uncles) paid one final visit, she became less conscious, and we were told that she did not have long. My father spent time alone with her, and then Conni and I sat on both sides of the bed holding each of her hands. I had her favorite music playing on my iPod from a playlist I had created called "Mom," and we spoke every possible positive affirmation we could think of about her life and taking care of the family so she could be reassured and at peace. The connection was powerful, but the inevitable would have to take its course, as it always must.

149

She passed that night, but the interconnectedness of everything continued to reverberate inside me. All of our experiences are different, and most departures of loved ones are sudden and without warning, which is an indication of how we must live our every waking moment with a sense of heightened sensitivity and gratitude. If we do not nurture a new state of consciousness that periodically "sees in time," then we remain trapped in a very small, ego-centered, me-based world. A higher state of consciousness longs to connect to higher places in itself and then to the events of the outside world. In my case, I found most of the inner terrain of egoistic reactions to the world boring, predictable, and downright illogical. I felt restless by these autopilot reactions to life and wanted new vistas, new understanding, and more responsibility to create a new interconnectedness within myself. In other words, I did not welcome being normal.

A final experience relative to the grief that my mother's passing gifted to me is also about connections. Over the years, she had sent me numerous cards and sometimes wrote notes to me in the inside sleeve. I saved some of these cards and kept them in a drawer that I knew would someday serve as a reaffirmation and comfort to console me when missing her. I now have a few of these cards in my office and glance at them next to pictures of her that again trigger these same deep connections we had throughout her life and those special moments we shared. She also gave me a strange little statue of a duck that I placed in front of our house. Every time I see this duck, I feel warmth pass through me *that feels* as if she is there. These experiences are all because of *connections, connections, and connections*. These conscious moments are lightning fast. I do not lament, stew, and dwell in self-pity in these moments. This is not a matter of emotionally suffering over loss as much as it is celebrating our existence and using these feelings to empower and grow. In such moments, sadness starts to fill my heart, but love, along with higher consciousness, rushes in to vanquish suffering. Cursing life for loss has no place in these psychological states, although for a time they are unavoidable and must play out. As I have tried to encourage in this book, it is vital that we think and ponder about the nature of this life but also pay close attention to the states that transcend time. A memory is one thing, an emotion is another, *and the conscious connection of thought, emotion, and consciousness together is yet an entirely new dimension*. These states and transformations are connected to the concept of neuralizing, which I mentioned earlier—remembering something without thinking about it. In other words, the impression of the duck triggers a sad feeling of loss, but consciousness does not *think about it*, meaning it does not dwell negatively. All this happens at an extraordinary speed in our body and consciousness. These are higher or more preferred ways to process events. The point is to direct a higher order of energy through our being and live from a slightly different level. There are certainly times when grief must express itself in all its fullness—crying and overwhelming sadness—but learning to use the highest connections that occurred *during life* elevates our current state and ensures that we include our loved ones in the life we now lead without them. It allows them to help us be happy and enables us to go on without them. It is always reassuring to ask ourselves in time of grief: *Would the person who passed want me to honor their life by contributing and doing good in life—and if so, how? Am I acting and being in a way that would make them proud that they spent their life with me?*

Grieving can be torture and can be existentially crippling if we do not make the effort to use the connections we have in our life and memory of that person to live our life to its highest potential. I found it very useful to replay my best memories and create a healthy mental dialogue with that person, especially when I realized that there is no one to stop me; it is *my* mind.

Strangely, Nancy had a very similar moment in hospice with her father, Vincent Latella. I was there when she experienced it, and it was also a moment of higher conscious energy that came through at an unexpected moment that marked time universally. In her case, her father was ninety-one years old and had an indomitable spirit to live. He had overcome many illnesses, heart surgeries, and physical debilitations for over a decade before being moved to hospice. Nancy's entire family was with him all the way, supporting him with love, guidance, and care as they battled one hurdle after another. On the night before he passed, Nancy and I were with him in his hospice room. He was heavily sedated in an unconscious state because we had also lost mental contact with him. That night, quite suddenly, he became filled with a tremendous surge of energy. Still not mentally coherent, he physically got out of the bed and could not be constrained as he moved around the room with determination and uncharacteristic force. I did my best to make sure he didn't hurt himself. It was a harrowing few minutes because he was speaking to himself with words that were unintelligible. Finally, he sat on the edge of his bed. I was at the door watching, and he, like my mother, suddenly, *in the stillness of time*, looked into Nancy's eyes and put two fingers under her chin as if to tickle her. Suddenly it was as if all disease, time, and suffering were lifted. A transference of similar profound, timeless love and gratitude filled them both. Again, without words, the moment became eternal. He then reclined into his bed and drifted into unconsciousness before passing away hours later.

He, like my mother who gave us the statue of a duck, gave us a small garden statue of a rabbit, which is also on our front lawn. I added a small flag with his favorite birds (two red cardinals), and they both send that same instantaneous transference of energy every time we glance at them. If ever possible, giving a loved one a special remembrance in the form of a gift (as mentioned earlier relative to the gift my sister-in-law, Gail, gave to me of the stone that read "Follow your Dreams"), no matter what it is, can be an almost supernatural event that brings their spirit back to us in subtle and extraordinary moments. Of course, *we have to raise our consciousness to a frequency that can receive it*. Remaining connected to past loved ones in a healthy and empowering way is a transcendental act that creates a positive mental web of energy. To this end, a good friend of ours, Patty Freudenberg, recently created a website and app called Miss-U-Gram that offers people who are grieving an opportunity to pay tribute and honor loved ones, to help people cope with loss. This is again an example of how our consciousness is evolving on a collective level, adding new ways to connect in a positive manner even in the face of adversity through loss. Again, it is literal hell to not work to elevate oneself in times of deep tragedy and loss and perhaps the single most difficult thing we ever do.

Lastly, I wanted to reference an example of what I consider one of the highest transformative practices one can apply relative toward working through grief. It is an insight that Joe Biden encouraged in his book, *Promise Me, Dad*. After losing his Wife and one year old daughter in a car accident, and then later in his life, losing his son Beau to brain cancer (three of the most unthinkable losses one can sustain), he said that one must reach a point in one's grieving that, when you think and remember those you lost, you experience *"a smile before a tear"*. In other words, *feel* the love, gratitude, joy, and warm memories of our lost ones over our own self pity, loneliness, and heartbreaking despair; after all, *they* are the ones that are no longer here. To celebrate *their* lives and honor *them*, raises the collective consciousness of humanity as a whole and consoles our heart and mind serving to heal and help us to press on with our lives.

The key to relating stories like these has to do with conscious evolution and new ways of transforming energy. We can enrich our lives by consciously activating higher energies and participating in this journey through life with a more proactive and intentional recourse—using the experiences we have cherished, valued, and loved to forge positive continuity not only for ourselves but for life. These experiences don't have to be as stark as the ones I've told. We all have thousands of moments to connect to and enjoy. They also do not have to be only during trauma and end of life. When neuralizing is done correctly, it is a creative and living process that each one of us can uniquely apply to our lives. We all have our own histories to contemplate and ponder with gratitude and openness. When we are open to growth, fresh and powerful energy is unleashed that helps us make these connections. From my perspective, these experiences need to be privately harvested and cultivated and not thoughtlessly keyed into phones and poured through Twitter, Instagram, and Facebook. While there is enjoyment, fun, and value to social media (I am not condemning it), there is a deeper level of communication that is far more enriching to our personal self that needs our attention. Today, the speed of communication on the external level is making self-reflection less enticing. People are locked into the narrative from social media and therefore have less chance of noticing the silk of a spider, the flight of a housefly, or the fact that their own consciousness longs to grow and expand individually.

Open Wrap-Up ... Open Vision ... Open Future ...

Ultimately, my book has been about one extraordinary phenomenon— *being alive, together in conscious connection*. We've explored conscious evolution and the extraordinary power of Kundalini energy, which encompasses the dizzying and bewildering infinitude of creativity and the bioelectrical reality that underlies and empowers it. I have made a point of emphasizing the cellular and physical dimension of the miracle of life and the promising potential that can result from an alignment with its natural genius. As human beings, we exemplify the highest, most complex, and most recent incarnation of a four-billion-year history, which is an astonishing fact. We embody all the wisdom of creation that is crystallizing now in a place in time where it is our responsibility to take the baton of life to the next stage of evolution. Throughout this book, I have tried to communicate the sense of gratitude and awe that inspired my journey that I felt deserved expression. The spirit of life is the very intelligent electricity that runs through every microorganism, plant, animal, and human, and each is a celebration of existence in its own right. Life strives, grows, and expands through the intelligent connections it forges, and our evolving ability to connect directly to them is all part of this grand and supreme design. The best way to see this is to fall completely silent; observe existence without words—even if for a few seconds—and look without mental noise, imbecilic voices, and preposterous baseless worries.

Consider how words can wreak havoc and how plants and animals live in the wonderful silence of action and have no mind to impose conflict, doubt, guilt, and stress.

Consider how the vast majority of life is benevolent by tuning into nature and watching her in her purest and most brilliant forms as they exist without toil and take even death with unconditional acceptance and peace.

Take a second and appreciate the invisible consciousness you are as you read these words and what an absolute miracle it is that you can think, love, appreciate, and live this life so nonchalantly when there is nothing simple about it. It is simply glorious that we are alive!

I understand that I have repeated, sometimes even word for word, certain ideas throughout this book, but it has been purposeful and with good reason. Most of us, including myself, enjoy reveling in the insights, visions, and ideals like the ones I have presented. I understand that it's difficult, if not impossible, to remember and apply higher ideas while absorbed and locked in the crossfire of physical, emotional, and egoistic reactions to the ordeals of everyday life. I specifically told my story of being a salesman in New York City while searching for transformation through Kundalini to provide a living sample of an effort quietly and secretly made in an otherwise commonplace and mundane life. I hope that it has been clear that an escalation of higher consciousness demands a new and different way of processing and perceiving in order not to get lost in the daily, transient minutiae of life, including the relatively serious parts.

We need healthier bodies, access to higher emotions, and disciplined use of reason and logic aimed at the collective good. We might want to consider our creative ingenuity as an inner spiritual war machine to combat our own lower nature, because this inner work can be difficult. It's is easy to give up, not care, or surrender. It is also easy to get down, depressed, and discouraged - *and worst of all cynical*. It is much harder to march forward and work for and with life to evolve and grow. We must remember that we really don't have a choice (if you seek higher experience)—the moment we choose cynical pessimism we contract instant negative karma—we, our precious consciousness—loses. It is also gravely important that we do *not* turn from the perennial wisdom of life's highest manifestations through scripture, art, music, and all fields, including science and technology. If we can read the teachings of a Buddha or Jesus (or any other being of higher consciousness) and not be inspired by them as advanced incarnations of nature, then we will not rise to higher levels. If we cannot appreciate the wisdom from poets, geniuses, and gifted human beings, then we have cut ourselves off from the very source that our own creation has stemmed from. Life is vibrating with intelligence in every conceivable living thing or subjective mental position— even those that we despise, reject, and hate. Such ugly manifestations of life are always steps in our evolution and never isolated evil. Our living and growing fabric longs for a level of consciousness that is active as opposed to stagnant. We ought to ask ourselves whether we are proactively managing our own being. Are we *upgrading ourselves* the way we upgrade our phones, computers, software, roads, and bridges? Do we have a new version of our self in production with more advanced features than we have today? If we are verbally attacked, is there a part of us that remains aware and conscious before launching an irrational and violent defense? This is the reality of what it means to do work on ourselves. Reading books and attending retreats will not rewire our behavior. *We have to do the work, or else remain childish and use escape as opposed to inner retaliation and revolution.*

I have honed into nature because no matter what our race, religion, creed, birthplace, or personal condition, we cannot question the cunning intelligence that underlies nature and the utter unquestionable integrity of her manifestations. It is compelling that consciousness derives from nature and therefore is its very home and surroundings. I have found that a serene inner comfort and inconceivable wealth of wisdom flows directly from this connection to nature and hopefully is shared by others. Nature, by tapping directly into the perceivable, tangible, and measurable intelligence, provides considerable security and calm fortitude while being enlightening and empowering. In a recent trip we took to Barcelona Spain, Nancy and I toured the Sagrada Familia, a stupefying cathedral that combines nature's genius, human genius, artistic genius, and divine inspiration all in one collective masterpiece (if we are not galvanized by such miracles as this cathedral, we need to take our pulses). These wondrous creations must continue to inspire our deepest meaning and purpose *and remind us* of who and what we are. I hope that by walking with me through my search for transformation, you have felt the same spiritual energy and intellectual insight of life's endless creativity; that you felt encouraged by an exciting inner world of revelation and expansion.

In closing, I want to acknowledge and thank you, my reader, for sharing your personal consciousness with mine for the time spent reading this book. I am not writing as a teacher or one with an established reputation in any field other than my personal life. I do not pretend to be an expert in consciousness, energy, or evolution. I am not trying to convince anyone to follow any path—*except one's own.* It is your own personal energetic evolution and revolution you must wage *in your-self* that has long term relevance. I have made my living and supported my family as a salesman in New York City and have relished the inner opportunities that life has afforded me. I am appreciative most of all for a life that has taught me a very profound lesson that, if put into words, would sound something like this:

If *you cannot connect everything, you cannot connect anything—rightly.*

The key prize is just that: *connecting everything.* Living this way enlivens, stirs, provokes, and intrigues the energetic spirit. Of course, no human can connect everything, but that is what makes it so much *fun.* Enjoy!

POSTSCRIPT

When I set out to write a book, I had several aggressive goals in mind. As the book took shape, it became clear that some of these goals would go either untouched or only briefly referenced. A deep part of me felt like this effort would not be complete if I did not address a few of the teachers, influences, and ideas that I felt deserved further clarification or mention. I also knew that some readers may not have an interest in a certain level of detail, while others might. Thus I resolved to offer this postscript to anyone who may want a few further reflections on these influences and ideas. I condensed them down to eight. The purpose is to fill out enough detail to provide direction into further study or exploration. This postscript helps me complete my vision of the total purpose of writing and publishing this book.

I. Gopi Krishna's Vision of Kundalini Energy as the Mechanism behind Evolution

Gopi Krishna lived from 1903 to 1984. He was an Indian mystic and teacher who experienced and delivered one of the most elaborate and profound Kundalini awakenings ever recorded in his book *Kundalini: The Evolutionary Energy in Man*. After this initial landmark book, he subsequently wrote sixteen more books and spoke and gave talks on the subject until the end of his life. In addition to his contribution to the experience and mystery of Kundalini, his deeper teaching was that this energy was the super intelligence behind all creation and was the true driver of all life. He strongly suggested the profound idea that the human brain is in a continual state of evolution and that life has an innate target, which higher consciousness is striving and moving toward. He also emphasized the biological aspect of this experience and stayed clear of mental fantasy, conceptual ideas, and dreamy theory. For him, the evidence was in the observable reality before our eyes, but he argued that science, as advanced and useful as it is, has not yet devised the future science necessary to better understand the nature and action of this energy. He urged that Kundalini be researched and studied, which he admitted will be a very difficult task but an inevitable part of our future. I would be remiss if I did not include a few quotes from his writings that I have highlighted, cherished, and returned to over and over since I first read them almost forty years ago. Pay close attention to the level of consciousness and stark and clear authoritative understanding of Kundalini he writes from. He, of course, is speaking directly about Kundalini energy in the following passages:

> "I found that the luminous current was acting with full knowledge of the task it had to perform and functioned in complete harmony with the bodily organs, knowing their strength and weakness, obeying its own laws and acting with a superior intelligence beyond my comprehension. The living fire, invisible to everyone else, darted here and there as if guided unerringly by a master-mind which knew the position of each vein and artery and each nerve fiber, and decided instantaneously what it had to do at the least sign of a hitch or disturbance in any organ." (*Kundalini: The Evolutionary Energy in Man*, Gopi Krishna)

> "The whole region from the throat to the base of the spine now becomes the operating theater of a radiant form of psychic energy which darts here and there along the nerves, like a streak of lightning, in a manner extremely bewildering and satisfying to the observer. But there is absolutely no doubt that the movement of the luminous current is governed by a Super Intelligence which regulates its activity according to the moment to moment varying needs of the organism". (*In the Wake of Awakening*, Gopi Krishna)

In these two short excerpts, consider again the fact that the super intelligence is really the total gene pool of life itself, which, as referenced in my book, is ancient and accessing blueprints of extraordinary and proven success in nature. This again is literal and real; nature couldn't be more real.

2. Kundalini Energy and Its Place in the Future of Humanity

When I first conceived of the idea to write a book, it was going to be solely about Kundalini energy. Shortly after I started writing formally about Kundalini, I realized it was not possible to discuss Kundalini without speaking in depth about consciousness, because it was clear that they were the same thing. Separating Kundalini from consciousness would be like separating heat and light from fire. The obvious challenge is that it is not well known in our part of the world, and it has been confused with many concepts and ideas that have rendered the entire phenomenon as either an occult concept or a bizarre anomaly with little scientific backing and integrity. Most people do not think about the energy of the body and whether there is a science to it. We think about the health of our organs and systems but not about the energy that animates the living body as a whole. Many people who get treated with acupuncture and other energy-oriented health treatments don't really ponder the underlying science and concepts of energy. Gopi Krishna strongly urged research into Kundalini because he considered it real enough to be studied by science but admitted and I concur, that such research would be very difficult for many reasons. My personal perspective on this matter is that we need to differentiate what exactly we mean by Kundalini and purge misconceptions and fantasy as much as possible before we move on to research. We also need to connect this concept of Kundalini with the growing popularity of all the energy-based health treatments as well at such popular physical practices like yoga, meditation, and Tai Chi. The question comes down to, what is the full potential of life through humanity, given the boundless capabilities we see in nature and what we have seen already in humanity? If in fact there is an evolving energy of conscious evolution, it must and has to have a science to it.

3. Jan Cox

Jan Cox was a teacher of higher consciousness from Atlanta who was unique beyond measure and lived from 1937 to 2005. As mentioned earlier, he became a profound influence on me in my early twenties. I met him personally twice briefly and connected via emails for about three years before he passed in 2005. He taught a group of interested students for more than forty years, delivered four books (and two transcripts), gave more than three thousand talks, and offered additional voluminous writings that are available through his website and are maintained today by a group of dedicated students. Jan's teachings were largely disseminated through his talks to groups of people in different states, as he fully understood that his teachings were not for the masses but for a specific type of person. He in no way tried to proselytize his teachings and left the onus of responsibility of attracting interested people to the students who valued his teaching.

I wouldn't and couldn't begin to explain his teachings in these short paragraphs but urge any interested readers to access his website (Jancox. com). He authored many ideas that were couched in his unique perspective, all having to do with consciousness. While I personally became thoroughly immersed and fascinated with his teachings, I wanted to be sure that a few of his ideas were referenced and credited clearly to him. The key idea that I referenced in the introduction was that *life itself is alive*. That it is a discrete and viable living entity that is living and growing and most specifically through humanity now. The idea has the extraordinary breadth that extends directly into the very processing of information and impressions that can and does lead to new ways of ingesting life and our existence. From this view, everything is in the process and nothing is static. Life and consciousness must remain on the move and never stare at anything too long, or else our consciousness stagnates and suffers. I specifically and only briefly fleshed out one idea of his called *neuralizing* because it reflects how our consciousness can begin to operate in a new way, at a different speed, and requires a comprehensive momentum to experience and profitably apply correctly. As mentioned above, his writings, insights, and perspectives are astutely made available on his website for further perusal.

4. Esoteric Knowledge, Gurdjieff, and Maurice Nicoll

I intentionally defined the word "esoteric" toward the very end of the book because everything I have written is understood to be of interest ultimately to a few people relative to the masses. Esoteric does not mean superior; it means tending to the few. On a planet where there are just over seven billion people in 2019, a few can mean millions, thousands, or hundreds. Most people are largely set in their ways and will automatically react from what is familiar rather than explore and venture into unknown and unchartered territory. It's basic human nature, and there is absolutely nothing wrong with it; matter of fact, it needs and has to be that way. The idea of esoteric knowledge has been interwoven in human history for thousands of years and can be identified in virtually every philosophy and religion. The main differentiator in terms of spirituality, energy, and consciousness is that the esoteric teachings are more about what is internal to a person and far less about the external world of events. This is a very deep and fascinating world for people who are drawn to it. The deepest teaching of an esoteric perspective is that everything taught by the spiritual masters was directed at the internal world. To turn the other cheek is meant to internally turn the other cheek when observing and become aware *of one's own nature*—to transcend self-hate and not judge yourself negatively. To not engage in a self-berating narrative against oneself but to directly welcome, encompass, understand, and grow from one's own inner hostility. Such a practice would generate positive energy that then flows out into the world. A person who seeks to take the "log out of one's own eye" before they seek to take the "speck of out their brother's" conveys deep inner meaning in that a person who becomes sincerely self-aware must always look for how they are not aware of themselves and stop looking outwardly at others by blaming, judging, and criticizing. What is both confounding and profound is that while esoteric teachings are only about one's inner world, the exact same teachings can be applied to the external world and make perfect sense from a certain level of consciousness. This is probably not an accident but not for me to say.

This idea alone can warrant endless dialogue, pondering, and revelation, but I wanted to mention it in the postscript because it is vital to understanding what I have written. George Gurdjieff (1855–1949) was the influence who impacted me and whom I referenced in the book, but it was his two prominent students, PD Ouspensky (1878–1947) and Maurice Nicoll (1884–1953), who conveyed the teachings to me more clearly and practically through their books. They, along with a few others, articulated the concept of esoteric conscious evolution in a way that I assimilated and applied throughout the journey and years reflected in this book.

5. Krishnamurti and Eckhart Tolle

These two teachers and influences I grouped together only because they are the most recently added teachers to my interest and influences. Although Krishnamurti (1885–1986) taught throughout most of his life and was highly active during the early part of my own involvement in esoteric knowledge, I did not start studying and reading his work until the last ten years or so. As I briefly mentioned in the book, Krishnamurti pleaded that people *think for themselves* and not receive information in a passive state. He was not content simply passing his understanding to groups of people; he would often pause and ask if anyone was listening and thinking about the words that were coming from his mouth. He would get visibly upset (with intention), knowing that people were just blindly following his narrative without participating with their own consciousness. He clearly felt that he was wasting his time if he was talking *at people* not *with people* and often begin his talks by insisting that the audience think and ponder *with him* and *share* the experience of inner expansion.

Eckhart Tolle is the most widely read and popular teacher that I have embraced. Eckhart is extraordinary on many levels and is conveying, from my perspective, an esoteric understanding to probably the largest audience, while still living, that I have ever seen. In addition to reading all of his books, I have been a member of his online membership on his website since it began and have attended retreats and talks. Again, it is not the purpose of this postscript to explain his teachings because it is all readily available to an interested seeker online and through his writings. It is far more powerful coming directly from him. I would only say relative to the context of this book that his consciousness is clearly activated on a very high level, and he has been speaking about the next level of human consciousness dawning and beginning to flower into a new stage. I can go on at length regarding his teaching, but again, that is not the purpose here. The singular idea that resonates in all these teachings, and most essentially in Eckhart's, is how life is evolving through humanity and that there is in fact a next level of consciousness forming that will encompass, transcend, and surpass thought as we relate to thought today. His teachings continue to flourish on many fronts circa 2019, and I strongly urge that an interested reader approach the totality of his work to gain a very profound and comprehensive understanding, as opposed to any form of book knowledge.

6. Alex Grey and Art

I am not a sophisticated art lover and actually know very little about art. I was always fascinated by the human attribute of being a skilled artist, no matter what form it takes—painting, sculpture, and so on. The level of precision, design, and imagination is striking, and once again, we need to question how and why humanity has such an innate gift. As one would imagine after reading my perspective on life, humanity is life's current medium of expression, and if we look at life itself as an artist, we should stand back and let our jaw drop. The cosmos, earth, and life itself is stunning when you look at it as artwork. If you feel so inclined and do not know of Alex Grey, then I implore a web search of his art work. It should be quite clear, if you read my book, why his visionary genius struck me so deeply. I couldn't imagine a more perfect rendition of how higher energy, life's miraculous nature, and consciousness are inseparably intertwined in all creation than the art of Alex Grey (and his wife, Alyson Grey's, art as well). The Greys' have and are creating an entire dimension around their work that can be researched on their website (alexgrey.com) and by researching their Chapel of Sacred Mirrors (COSM), which is in Upstate New York. Pay also close attention to anything he has written in his books in how his consciousness reflects the level of art his hand produces. It is profound to behold when the evolution of art and the evolution of consciousness are aligned in one being. This is a major thrust of my book. The point I want to emphasize is that we are all artists in the manner and way we conduct our lives. Everything we *are* is our art, from how we treat others, to how we treat ourselves, to how we nurture animals and the environment, to how we perform our jobs, rear our children, help our friends, or are just being pleasant and kind to others. It is all about how we align our inner lives to the collective conscious intelligence of life itself.

7. Michael Mollura

I mentioned my brother, Michael Mollura, when I referenced that he scored a movie called *Heal*. Michael is a musician and psychologist who scored the movies *Climate Refugees, Awake: The Life of Yogananda, The Highest Pass, Hare Krishna, Hot Coffee, and Heal*. He most recently has been introducing very profound work in the area of dreams and dream music therapy and recently completed a successful workshop at the Esalen Inspirational Film Festival where he introduced his Dream Music Master Class. He offers new and profound insight while he also takes on new projects that combine music soundtracks, spiritual revelation, and one-to-one therapy and couching. For more information visit ww.drmichaelmollura.com, or www.michaelmolluramusic.com.

8. Existence, Nature, and Life

The purpose of this postscript has been to reference standout influences and teachers, but the greatest of all, and the one that I hope touched the reader, is that of the utter miracle of existence, nature, and life. An emotional appreciation for the fact that we all have our own temporal yet astounding existence is essential to an inner search that can drive an impetus to do everything we can to grow and evolve internally. People whose consciousness is not drawn at least to a small part to the mystery of life miss out on a most intriguing and potentially enriching synergy of the living energies of a more conscious life. What fascinates me most is that every single individual across the entire breadth of humanity has a unique opportunity to experience and engage life from a pricelessly personal and individualistic view. Nobody shares the exact family, the exact past, the exact talents, the exact interests. It is absolutely impossible, and that is everyone's unique ticket to their personal evolution that contributes to the collective growth of life. This wonderful reality can come into focus only when our attention silently peruses existence, the earth, and nature with a sense of gratitude and appreciation. Our silent consciousness needs to come home to itself and unconditionally accept not with mental logic but with something much higher and more astounding. The one sincere question for the few people who are drawn to this dimension is whether that person feels and sees a deeply interwoven integrity to life and spends the precious and miraculous moments they live by honoring it and serving its long-term good. The most dangerous minds in the universe are those that have stopped evolving and creating. For me, while we must pursue our most perfect life, ultimately we must surrender it to the enduring and supreme collective consciousness and a future we cannot know with our mortal mind. It makes sense to live for the long-term good of life itself, no matter what our individual beliefs. To serve this higher purpose uplifts, encourages, and calms our spirit and helps us pass peacefully into our unknowable future—always with a sense of adventure.

Printed in the United States
By Bookmasters